ℒENT *and* ℰASTER 𝒲ISDOM
—— *from* ——
POPE FRANCIS

John Cleary

Imprimi Potest:
Stephen T. Rehrauer, CSsR, Provincial, Denver Province, the Redemptorists

Published by Liguori Publications, Liguori, Missouri 63057
To order, visit Liguori.org or call 800-325-9521.

Library of Congress Cataloging-in-Publication Data

Cleary, John J.
   Lent and Easter wisdom from Pope Francis / John Cleary.
     pages cm
   ISBN 978-0-7648-2647-4
   1. Lent—Prayers and devotions. 2. Easter—Prayers and devotions.
   3. Catholic Church—Prayers and devotions. 4. Francis, Pope, 1936—Quotations.
   I. Title.
   BX2170.L4C54 2015
   242'.34—dc23
                              2015020868

p ISBN 978-0-7648-2647-4
e ISBN 978-0-7648-7079-8

Liguori Publications, a nonprofit corporation, is an apostolate of the Redemptorists. To learn more about the Redemptorists, visit Redemptorists.com.

Printed in the United States of America
19 18 17 16 15 / 5 4 3 2 1
First Edition

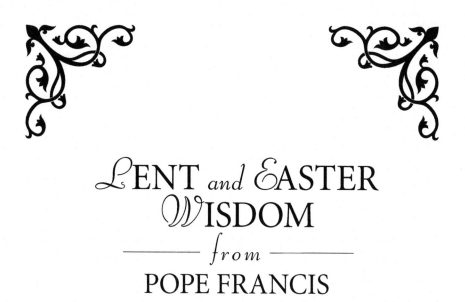

LENT and EASTER WISDOM

—— from ——
POPE FRANCIS

Daily Scripture and Prayers Together
With Pope Francis' Own Words

John Cleary

Liguori

Dedication

For my children, Joseph and Elizabeth, who fill my life with
joy; for my parents, John and Carol Cleary, who stand with me
through better and worse; and for my sister Cathy and brother
Ryan, whose love I feel even from miles and miles away.

$\mathcal{C}$ontents

$\mathscr{P}$reface

A Path for Lent and Easter

$\mathscr{I}$t seems to me that our perception of the Lenten journey to Easter still consists of archaic remnants of our shared Judeo-Christian history. Beating our breast, rolling around in ashes, and wearing sackcloth, all while wailing about our sins. While this list of self-abasement for our sins still has its place, we should not lose sight of the reason we do these things. We fast to commemorate the fasting of Jesus during his temptation in the desert and to experience solidarity with the poor and hungry, among other reasons. We also fast to display our total reliance on God the Father, provider of all things, from life to freedom to manna in the desert to the completion of salvation and the defeat of death through the sacrifice of his Son, our Lord Jesus Christ.

So should we be celebrating sin during the season of Lent? That might be going a step or two too far. We are called to contemplate and feel the weight of guilt about those thoughts and actions that break the chain of grace linking us to God. The sacrament of reconciliation should always be a frequent experience for every Catholic, but perhaps even more so during Lent. Have you ever heard the metaphor that when we break the rope between God and us by sinning, our reconciliation to God moves the Father to tie the loose ends of that rope into a knot, drawing us closer to him and strengthening the bond between us even more? That's the positive perspective on sinning, but only when it is followed by reconciliation.

Saints Thérèse of Lisieux and Francis of Assisi, perhaps the two most beloved saints of the last century, both understood humility—that is, their place in the presence of the Father as one of his beloved creatures. Saint Francis abandoned all material things for his full reliance on God. Saint Thérèse, as her main goal in life, wanted to be as close to Jesus as possible. During her last years of immense suffering, Thérèse took great pleasure in the fact that her pain was further uniting her with Jesus, who sanctified every aspect of human existence—including suffering—during his earthly ministry. Thérèse knew how little she was in the presence of the Lord, and she longed for something akin to the newly invented elevator of her time to raise her ever closer to her Savior. She committed herself to a way of life that immersed itself in the child-parent relationship of full dependence, trust, and humility.

Throughout this Lenten and Easter journey, we will explore the wellspring of full dependence on the Lord, trust in his will, and the generosity of his grace that serve as the hallmarks of the faith of Pope Francis. His spirituality—expressed herein in a variety of settings in Vatican City, unless otherwise noted—is a unique combination of all the best aspects of the Society of Jesus (self-discipline, asceticism, and austerity) and the deep faithfulness to humility and total reliance on God of St. Thérèse of Lisieux. The Holy Father is a great devotee of both of these saints. May the devout words of our beloved Francis guide us along our own path to greater nearness and devotion to our Savior, and may our loving Jesus draw us closer to him by his great and unfailing mercy. May we grow closer to him—not in spite of our sin but because we fall short and depend on his grace for a greater nearness; also, may we contemplate the salvific beauty of the great mystery of Jesus' resurrection.

Know also, dear readers, that your spiritual growth and welfare are committed to my own prayers as you proceed along this worthy Lenten and Easter journey.

John Cleary
St. Louis, 2015

$\mathcal{I}$ntroduction

$\mathcal{M}$ ost Catholics seem to be aware of the forty-day period before the feast of Easter. Lent, which comes from the Anglo-Saxon word *lencten*, meaning "spring," is a time marked by particular rituals, such as the reception of ashes on Ash Wednesday or the decision to give up French fries as a Lenten practice. But Lent is broader than just these practices, which seem to be left over from another era.

A Brief History of Lent

In the first three centuries of the Christian experience, preparation for the Easter feast usually covered a period of one or two days, perhaps a week at the most. Saint Irenaeus of Lyons even speaks of a forty-hour preparation for Easter.

The first reference to Lent as a period of forty days' preparation occurs in the teachings of the First Council of Nicaea in 325 and, by the end of the fourth century, a Lenten period of forty days was established and accepted.

In its early development, Lent quickly became associated with the sacrament of baptism, since Easter was the great baptismal feast. Those who were preparing to be baptized participated in the season of Lent in preparation for the reception of the sacrament of baptism. Eventually, those who were already baptized considered it important to join those candidates preparing for baptism in their preparations for Easter. The customs and practices of Lent as we know them today soon took hold.

LENT AS A JOURNEY

Lent is often portrayed as a journey, from one point in time to another. The concept of journey is obvious for those experiencing the Rite of Christian Initiation of Adults (RCIA), the program of baptismal preparation conducted in most parishes during the season of Lent.

But Lenten preparation is not limited to those who are preparing to be baptized and join the Church. For many Catholics, Lent is a journey that is measured from Ash Wednesday through Easter. But more accurately, Lent is measured from Ash Wednesday to the beginning of the period of time known as the Triduum.

Triduum begins after the Mass on Holy Thursday, continues through Good Friday, and concludes with the Easter Vigil on Holy Saturday. Lent officially ends with the proclamation of the *Exscultet*, "Rejoice O Heavenly Powers," during the Mass of Holy Saturday. By whatever yardstick the journey is measured, it is not only the period of time that is important but the essential experiences of the journey that are necessary for a full appreciation of what is being celebrated.

The Lenten journey is also a process of spiritual growth and presumes movement from one state of being to another. For example, some people may find themselves troubled and anxious at the beginning of Lent as a result of a life choice or an unanswered question, and at the end of Lent, they may fully expect a sense of conversion, a sense of peace, or simply understanding and acceptance. In this sense, Lent is a movement from one point of view to another or, perhaps, from one interpretation of life to another.

Scripture, psalms, prayers, rituals, practices, and penance are the components of the Lenten journey. Each component, tried and tested by years of tradition, is one of the engines that drives the season and which brings the weary traveler to the joys of Easter.

A popular understanding of Lent is that it is a time of penance during which people attempt to become more sensitive to the role of sin in their lives. Lenten sermons will speak of personal sin, coming to an awareness of the sins of others, the effect such sin might have, and, finally, the sin that can be found within our larger society and culture. Awareness of sin is balanced by an emphasis on the love and acceptance God has for humanity, despite the sinful condition in which we find ourselves.

The practice of meditation on the passion of the Lord emphasizes the awareness of sin and the need for penance. There is also an emphasis on the reception of the sacrament of reconciliation during Lent. Originally, the sacrament of reconciliation was celebrated before Lent began, with the penance imposed on Ash Wednesday and performed during the entire forty-day period.

SUMMONS TO PENITENTIAL LIVING

For forty days, we imitate the example of Jesus fasting and praying in the desert. It is time to center our attention on conversion. We are called to examine our lives and, through the practice of prayer, fasting, and works of charity, to conform our lives to Christ's. For some, this conversion will be a turning from sin to grace. For others, it will be a gracious turning toward the mystery of God in Christ. Whatever your pattern for observance this Lent, I hope this book will provide a useful support in the effort.

JOURNALING

For many of the days during this Lenten and Easter season, it is recommended that you have a notebook and pen available. The "Action" for the day will frequently involve a brief journal entry. Often, putting your thoughts to paper—actually seeing these ideas in your own handwriting—can have a more lasting emotional impact than simply calling a few ideas to mind when prompted and forgetting them soon after the fact. Writing out your responses to the questions asked during the "Lenten/Easter Action" portion of many of these days allows the reader to review, reflect, and revise his or her thinking on a particular spiritual topic. It allows for growth, and that's what this life is all about—constantly growing closer to and in deeper union with our Lord and Savior.

A Chronology of the Life of Pope Francis

December 17, 1936	Jorge Mario Bergoglio is born in Buenos Aires, Argentina, to Mario José Bergoglio, an Italian immigrant, and Regina Maria Sivori of Argentina.
December 1957	At age 21, he falls gravely ill; severe pneumonia is diagnosed and part of his right lung is removed. He recovers fully and decides to devote himself to the priesthood.
March 11, 1958	Enters the novitiate of the Society of Jesus
March 12, 1960	Takes his first vows as a Jesuit
1961–1963	Studies philosophy at San Miguel Seminary in Buenos Aires
1967–1970	Studies theology at San Miguel Seminary
December 13, 1969	Ordained priest
1973	Takes perpetual profession as Jesuit
1973–1979	Serves as superior of Jesuit province of Argentina and Uruguay
June 27, 1992	Fr. Jorge, as he is known, is ordained Auxiliary Bishop of Buenos Aires.
February 28, 1998	Installed as Archbishop of Buenos Aires
2001	Co-presides over Synod of Bishops
February 21, 2001	Elevated to cardinal
2005–2011	Serves as president, Argentine Bishops Conference
March 13, 2013	Elected 266th pope of the Catholic Church, he is the first Holy Father from the Americas, the first Jesuit, and the first to take the name Francis.
September 2015	Makes first papal visit to the United States, attending the 2015 World Meeting of Families in Philadelphia

PART I

~

READINGS *for* LENT

Day

1

Ash Wednesday
The Lord Seeks Conversion of Heart

"Rend your hearts and not your garments" (Joel 2:13).

These penetrating words of the Prophet Joel...[point] to conversion of heart as the chief characteristic of this season of grace. The prophetic appeal challenges all of us without exception, and it reminds us that conversion is not to be reduced to outward forms or to vague intentions, but engages and transforms one's entire existence beginning from the center of the person, from the conscience.

Francis' Homily at Holy Mass,
Blessing and Imposition of the Ashes,
Basilica of Santa Sabina, March 5, 2014

Scripture

The Pharisees saw this and said to his disciples, "Why does your teacher eat with tax collectors and sinners?" [Jesus] heard this and said, "Those who are well do not need a physician, but the sick do. Go and learn the meaning of the words, 'I desire mercy, not sacrifice.' I did not come to call the righteous but sinners."

MATTHEW 9:11–13

Prayer

Great and generous Lord, physician to our souls, you came to those who needed you the most. People with open hearts were drawn to you; nothing they were prescribed by the spiritual leaders of the time filled the emptiness inside. These people did not put on airs; they wanted to love you and they desired your love, compassion, and healing in return. Just as you gave yourself to those people during your earthly ministry, we ask that you give yourself to us today. This is all we ask. Amen.

Lenten Action

In your journal, write a response to this: In what ways do I find myself unfulfilled by the "answers" and "medicine" that the world offers? Why does worldliness fail to satisfy my hunger for union and intimacy with others? What can Jesus provide that satisfies the hunger I feel at my core? At what times in my life have I known this fulfillment? During what periods has it been lacking?

Day

2

Thursday After Ash Wednesday
Fasting Reminds Us of the Essential

*F*asting makes sense if it questions our security, and if it also leads to some benefit for others, if it helps us to cultivate the style of the Good Samaritan, who bends down to his brother in need and takes care of him. Fasting involves choosing a sober lifestyle; a way of life that does not waste, a way of life that does not "throw away." Fasting helps us to attune our hearts to the essential and to sharing.

FRANCIS' HOMILY AT HOLY MASS,
BLESSING AND IMPOSITION OF THE ASHES,
BASILICA OF SANTA SABINA, MARCH 5, 2014

SCRIPTURE

*When you fast, do not look gloomy like the hypocrites. They
neglect their appearance, so that they may appear to others to
be fasting. Amen, I say to you, they have received their reward.
But when you fast, anoint your head and wash your face, so that
you may not appear to be fasting, except to your Father who is
hidden. And your Father who sees what is hidden will repay you.*

MATTHEW 6:16–18

PRAYER

Loving God, who sees all and knows our every intention,
grace us with the desire to fast for the sake of deeper intimacy
with you and greater empathy with our brothers and sisters
who go to bed hungry every night. Allow our fasting to
help us understand the true value of sustenance. Help us
appreciate the gifts you give in a deeper way, even on those
occasions where we are left wanting more. May this deeper
union with you satisfy us beyond what mere food can
provide. Amen.

LENTEN ACTION

In your journal, write a response to this: Describe your experience
of fasting. How does fasting affect you from a spiritual point of
view? How does the practice affect your relationship with God?
How does it affect your understanding, appreciation, and empathy
with those who go without on a regular basis? How does fasting
shape your prayer life? How does the practice of fasting keep you
from taking what you have for granted?

$\mathcal{D}$ay

3

Friday After Ash Wednesday
Create Something New

$\mathcal{W}$ith its invitations to conversion, Lent comes providentially to awaken us, to rouse us from torpor, from the risk of moving forward by inertia. The exhortation which the Lord addresses to us through the prophet Joel is strong and clear: "Return to me with your whole heart" (Joel 2:12). Why must we return to God? Because something is not right in us, not right in society, in the Church and we need to change, to give it a new direction. And this is called needing to convert!

FRANCIS' HOMILY AT HOLY MASS,
BLESSING AND IMPOSITION OF THE ASHES,
BASILICA OF SANTA SABINA, MARCH 5, 2014

Scripture

A clean heart create for me, God;
renew within me a steadfast spirit.
Do not drive me from before your face,
nor take from me your holy spirit.
Restore to me the gladness of your salvation;
uphold me with a willing spirit.

PSALM 51:12–14

Prayer

Lord God, fashion within me a willing spirit, one that embraces the promise of Lent and its fulfillment of salvation on Easter Sunday. Wake me from my lethargy, from the apathy that insidiously seeps into my consciousness when I am preoccupied with lesser goods. You are the greatest good available. Move my heart, soften it, allow it to open and blossom to the promise of conversion that Lent affords us. I ask this in the name of the Word and the Resurrection, your Son, our Lord Jesus Christ. Amen.

Lenten Action

What are your goals for this Lent? As a child, and still as adults, we are often encouraged to give something up, but as we mature in our faith we should also add during Lent. Often, what's added is a clean heart acquired from the Father's grace that allows us to be sensitive to the needs of others, understanding and addressing their needs before tending to our own. What might you add to your spiritual exercises during this Lenten season?

Day

4

Saturday After Ash Wednesday
God's Love Transforms

*I*t was only in this way, by taking flesh, by sharing our humanity, that the knowledge proper to love could come to full fruition. For the light of love is born when our hearts are touched and we open ourselves to the interior presence of the beloved, who enables us to recognize his mystery....By his taking flesh and coming among us, Jesus has touched us, and through the sacraments he continues to touch us even today; transforming our hearts, he unceasingly enables us to acknowledge and acclaim him as the Son of God.

FRANCIS' ENCYCLICAL LETTER *LUMEN FIDEI*, 31, JUNE 29, 2013

SCRIPTURE

What was from the beginning,
what we have heard,
what we have seen with our eyes,
what we looked upon
and touched with our hands
concerns the Word of life[.]

1 JOHN 1:1

Prayer

Heavenly Father, by your generosity through the mystery of the Incarnation, your Son became man. The Word took on flesh and sanctified every aspect of our human experience. God ate with us, walked by our side, spoke with us, taught us, healed us, and forgave us. Everything human he blessed by his presence in the flesh so that, when we experience what he experienced, we enter into a human-divine bond with God, an intimacy that could never have occurred without the mystery of the Incarnation. We can only express our gratitude for this deep love and cherish the reality that the divine has transformed our humanity. Amen.

Lenten Action

By taking on our humanity through the mystery of the Incarnation, Jesus sanctified every facet of our existence, from the way we relate to one another, to the way we enter into intimacy in prayer with God, to the way we are able to express mercy and forgiveness to one another. When you reflect on the mystery of the Incarnation, what area of your humanity are you most thankful that Jesus has sanctified by becoming man?

Day

5

First Sunday of Lent
We Are Born Anew

ow does one become a member of this people? It is not through physical birth, but through a new birth....It is through Baptism that we are introduced into this people, through faith in Christ, a gift from God that must be nourished and cultivated throughout our life. Let us ask ourselves: how do I make this faith that I received in my Baptism grow?

FRANCIS, GENERAL AUDIENCE, ST. PETER'S SQUARE,
JUNE 12, 2013

SCRIPTURE

Thomas said to him, "Master, we do not know where you are going; how can we know the way?" Jesus said to him, "I am the way and the truth and the life. No one comes to the Father except through me."

JOHN 14:5–6

PRAYER

Jesus, my dearest and most intimate friend, I have experienced a new birth with you. If I was a baby when my baptism happened I may not remember it, or it might have been something I chose as an adult, but—nonetheless—I am born "from on high, from water and from the Spirit." I later confirmed this pledge through the sacrament and am ready to enter the kingdom of heaven after my life on earth is finished. And may I ask you this grace, my Lord? Transform my heart, humble it in the manner of a child's heart, that I may see with the eyes of a child, with eyes that trust, with eyes that constantly wonder in awe at your greatness and glory. Amen.

LENTEN ACTION

This exercise calls for an effort of memory. Recall portions of your childhood. Your first circus. First trip to a big-league baseball game. An early Christmas. Imagine your eyes, wide with wonder. You were naïve and every experience was new. Now you're older. Experiences that were once new and wondrous might seem stale. This does not mean you've lost the eyes of a child or the humility a child exudes in the encounter of a new experience. Pray on this. Ask God for freshness of heart, for new eyes, for humility. God will grace you with a child's eyes and you can experience his presence in everything again.

$\mathcal{D}$ay

6

Monday of the First Week of Lent
Knowing Our Place in Creation

$\mathcal{W}$e know that this increasingly artificial world would have us live in a culture of "doing," of the "useful," where we exclude God from our horizon without realizing it....Lent beckons us to "rouse ourselves," to remind ourselves that we are creatures, simply put, that we are not God. In the little daily scene, as I look at some of the power struggles to occupy spaces, I think: these people are playing God the Creator. They still have not realized that they are not God.

FRANCIS' HOMILY AT HOLY MASS,
BLESSING AND IMPOSITION OF THE ASHES,
BASILICA OF SANTA SABINA, MARCH 5, 2014

SCRIPTURE

Do nothing out of selfishness or out of vainglory; rather, humbly regard others as more important than yourselves, each looking out not for his own interests, but [also] everyone for those of others.

PHILIPPIANS 2:3–4

Prayer

Lord Jesus, you humbled yourself like no other by becoming man. If God—for love of the men and women he created—can humble himself in such a way, how should we live out our own lives? Grace me, loving God, to see my place in your creation, to humble myself in service to others just as you served the lowly. Am I any better than you that I should demand a greater place? Allow me to learn the humility that unites me to you for all eternity. Amen.

Lenten Action

In your journal, write a response to this: In what ways do I humble myself before my fellow brothers and sisters? How does Jesus inspire me to do this? Do I sometimes put on airs in the presence of others, talking myself up as someone more important than I am? Recall an example of when you did this. Why do I tend to behave this way at times? Is it insecurity, a feeling of inferiority, or a lack of self-esteem? Is it possible to maintain a strong sense of self-esteem and still be as humble as Jesus? What makes this practice so difficult at some points in my life and so effortless at others?

Day
7

Tuesday of the First Week of Lent
Give Genuinely

*T*he elements of this spiritual journey [are] prayer, fasting, and
almsgiving (see Matthew 6:1–6; 16–18). All three exclude the
need for appearances: what counts is not appearances; the value of
life does not depend on the approval of others or on success, but
on what we have inside us.

FRANCIS' HOMILY AT HOLY MASS,
BLESSING AND IMPOSITION OF THE ASHES,
BASILICA OF SANTA SABINA, MARCH 5, 2014

SCRIPTURE

*[But] take care not to perform righteous deeds in order
that people may see them; otherwise, you will have no
recompense from your heavenly Father. When you give
alms, do not blow a trumpet before you, as the hypocrites
do in the synagogues and in the streets to win the praise of
others. Amen, I say to you, they have received their reward.*

MATTHEW 6:1–2

PRAYER

Generous and loving Father, you give to us without counting the cost. You give so generously that you offered to us your only beloved Son, our Lord Jesus. Grace us, Father, with the ability to follow the example your Son modeled in his earthly ministry. When we give, let it be so natural, such a genuine part of who we are, that our left hand does not know what our right is doing. We ask this through your benevolent grace. Amen.

LENTEN ACTION

Spend ten minutes in quiet reflection and think about the various ways you give of yourself as a believer and follower of Jesus Christ. List these ways of giving in your journal. You can give monetarily, but try to call to mind the ways you give with the gifts God has graced you with. You might be someone who prays a lot; that is a great gift to impart to the Church. Perhaps you are an artist, a sympathetic ear/gifted listener, or a mediator between parties who are at odds with one another. List every gift you can think of, no matter how small, and offer up a prayer of gratitude.

Day

8

Wednesday of the First Week of Lent
Joseph Helped Jesus Grow

*B*eing a guardian is the distinctive trait of Joseph: Being
the guardian is his great mission....We look to Joseph as
the model educator, who watches over and accompanies Jesus as
he grows "in wisdom, age and grace," as the Gospel says. He was
not Jesus' father: the father of Jesus was God, but he was a father to
Jesus, he was a father to Jesus in order to help him grow. And how
did he help him grow? In wisdom, age, and grace.

FRANCIS' GENERAL AUDIENCE, ST. PETER'S SQUARE,
MARCH 19, 2014

SCRIPTURE

*Now may God himself, our Father, and our Lord Jesus direct
our way to you, and may the Lord make you increase and
abound in love for one another and for all, just as we have
for you[.]*

1 THESSALONIANS 3:11–12

PRAYER

Joseph, humble stepfather of Jesus, what an admirable example you make. First and foremost, the will of God was a priority in your life. You took Mary into your home, you followed the direction of the angel of the Lord, and you protected your family by departing for Egypt. You were a simple carpenter, a man devoted to a craft you passed along to your Son; a man devoted to your family, putting their needs ahead of your own. Joseph, help me to live by your example and put Jesus first in my life this Lent. Amen.

LENTEN ACTION

Looking back on your life, on the decisions you have made with and without the input of God's will, can you call to mind and write down two to three examples of moments when you had your mind made up to do something but then God's will intervened and you followed without question?

Do you have trouble giving up your earthly security to take a leap of faith in God? Is there an area of your life where you could be more open to God's will? How do you help those around you grow in their faith? How do you encourage others to follow God's will for their lives? Ask St. Joseph to intercede for you as you pray about these issues.

*D*ay

9

Thursday of the First Week of Lent
Joseph, Teacher of Wisdom

*J*oseph was for Jesus the example and the teacher of the wisdom that is nourished by the Word of God. We could ponder how Joseph formed the little Jesus to listen to the Sacred Scriptures, above all by accompanying him on Saturday to the Synagogue in Nazareth. Joseph accompanied Jesus so that he would listen to the Word of God in the Synagogue.

FRANCIS' GENERAL AUDIENCE, ST. PETER'S SQUARE,
MARCH 19, 2014

SCRIPTURE

Let the word of Christ dwell in you richly, as in all wisdom
you teach and admonish one another, singing psalms,
hymns, and spiritual songs with gratitude in your hearts
to God. And whatever you do, in word or in deed, do
everything in the name of the Lord Jesus, giving thanks to
God the Father through him.

COLOSSIANS 3:16–17

PRAYER

Lord, I know that wisdom means "the quality of having experience, knowledge, and good judgment," but how often I forget that you are the source of all wisdom! I sometimes view my increase in wisdom as simply being able to learn from my mistakes, as an exercise in trial and error reliant on my ability independent of you. Indeed, experience is a great teacher, but there is more to it than that. Just as Joseph formed the Child Jesus by taking him to hear the wisdom of the word of God proclaimed in the synagogue, so also do I learn wisdom from the word of God. Lord, grace me with the wisdom to seek you out in your word and not to rely only on my earthly knowledge and experiences. Amen.

LENTEN ACTION

In your journal, write down three areas of your life in which you have gained wisdom over the years. Examples could range from maturity in relationships (either personal or professional) to growth in expectations of certain people to a deeper understanding of your relationship with God. Choose a specific experience from your past when you acted with a lack of wisdom and then imagine how you would approach that situation today. What would stay the same? What would be different? How does this knowledge change your relationships with God and others? How can it guide your Lenten reflection?

$\mathcal{D}$ay

10

Friday of the First Week of Lent
Mary, Our Intercessor

$\mathcal{M}$ary, help us to entrust ourselves fully to him and to believe in his love, especially at times of trial, beneath the shadow of the cross, when our faith is called to mature. Sow in our faith the joy of the Risen One. Remind us that those who believe are never alone. Teach us to see all things with the eyes of Jesus, that he may be light for our path. And may this light of faith always increase in us, until the dawn of that undying day which is Christ himself, your Son, our Lord!

FRANCIS' ENCYCLICAL LETTER *LUMEN FIDEI*, 60,
JUNE 29, 2013

Scripture

And Mary said:

"My soul proclaims the greatness of the Lord;
    my spirit rejoices in God my savior.
For he has looked upon his handmaid's lowliness;
    behold, from now on will all ages call me blessed.
The Mighty One has done great things for me,
    and holy is his name.
His mercy is from age to age
    to those who fear him."

LUKE 1:46–50

Prayer

Mary, Mother of God, we ask that you inspire us to see the world through the eyes of God this Lent. These attributes of desire, trust, and belief are hallmarks of your relationship with the Father, Blessed Virgin, and who better to appeal to as intercessor in seeking them for own personal, intimate relationship with the divine? In your Magnificat you sum up what a believer aspires to be—gracious, humble, and willing. Help us to behave in a like manner when presented with the Father's will for us. Amen.

LENTEN ACTION

Reread the Magnificat and reflect on the deep humility Mary expresses, the heartfelt desire to serve God wholly and completely. Mary was the vessel handpicked by the Father for a very unique purpose. We also have a unique purpose for which God has selected us. It is up to us to be openhearted, humble, and willing enough to say "yes" to his will and follow where he leads. When we avoid doing God's will, all we do is get caught up in the throes of anxiety and doubt, tools the devil is pleased to use as a wedge between God and us. So pray to Mary for the resolve to give an immediate "yes" to what God asks of us. Only good can follow from this practice.

Day
11

Saturday of the First Week of Lent
Give Freely, Expect Nothing

*I*n almsgiving one gives something to someone [without expecting] anything in return. Gratuitousness should be one of the characteristics of the Christian, who, aware of having received everything from God gratuitously, that is, without any merit of his own, learns to give to others freely....Almsgiving helps us experience giving freely, which leads to freedom from the obsession of possessing, from the fear of losing what we have, from the sadness of one who does not wish to share his wealth with others.

FRANCIS' HOMILY AT HOLY MASS, BASILICA OF SANTA SABINA, MARCH 5, 2014

SCRIPTURE

When [Jesus] looked up he saw some wealthy people putting their offerings into the treasury and he noticed a poor widow putting in two small coins. He said, "I tell you truly, this poor widow put in more than all the rest; for those others have all made offerings from their surplus wealth, but she, from her poverty, has offered her whole livelihood."

LUKE 21:1–4

PRAYER

Generous Father of heartfelt giving, your deep and abiding love for us motivates a generosity beyond measure, a generosity without limits. Despite our sins you call us to repent and return to you time and again. Those who give from their surplus remain secure in their earthly possessions; but those who give everything display a faith that is totally reliant on you. Grace me to give as the widow did and may my reliance be always and only on you with the desire to love beyond worldliness. Amen.

LENTEN ACTION

In the next few days, make an effort to give more than you normally would to a person in need or to a cause that appeals to you. Sacrifice a greater amount than you normally would for the sake of closer intimacy to the heart of the Gospel (feeding the hungry, clothing the naked, providing housing for the homeless or orphaned children, and so on). It doesn't have to be an exorbitant amount, just enough to sacrifice a daily luxury (like a lunch out or your morning coffee). Give more than you normally would and offer it up with a prayer to God.

$\mathcal{D}$ay
12

Second Sunday of Lent
Jesus Came in Poverty

$\mathcal{B}$y making himself poor, Jesus did not seek poverty for its own sake but, as St. Paul says, "that by his poverty you might become rich." This is no mere play on words or a catch phrase. Rather, it sums up God's logic, the logic of love, the logic of the incarnation and the cross....When Jesus stepped into the waters of the Jordan and was baptized by John the Baptist, he did so not because he was in need of repentance, or conversion; he did it to be among people who need forgiveness, among us sinners, and to take upon himself the burden of our sins.

FRANCIS' LENTEN MESSAGE, 2014

SCRIPTURE

I say this not by way of command, but to test the genuineness of your love by your concern for others. For you know the gracious act of our Lord Jesus Christ, that for your sake he became poor although he was rich, so that by his poverty you might become rich.

2 CORINTHIANS 8:8–9

Prayer

Lord Jesus Christ, king of heaven, you humbled yourself to meet us where we were, mired in our state of poverty. This is how you established our freedom. What a mystery! I would think your riches and freedom would come to me from above, raining down on us from on high, not from a plane of equality, a state of poverty. It is only by your grace. You meet us where we are. We cannot come to you because we are incapable to crossing the breach. Only the God-man can do that, and how blessed am I that he deigns to lower himself and meet me where I am. Praise God! Amen!

Lenten Action

For today, attempt this exercise in imagination: Imagine you approach a park bench where a five-year-old child is seated. You sit beside him. You are dressed in blue jeans and a T-shirt, just like he is. When you talk to him about the wonderful places he'll go some day, you use small, uncomplicated words he can understand. He feels special because you are taking the time to talk to him on his level. We are that child in so many ways; God makes us feel special when he lowers himself to our place and speaks to us like he is one of us—because he is one of us.

$\mathcal{D}$ay
13

Monday of the Second Week of Lent
The Church Helps the Destitute

$\mathcal{M}$aterial destitution is what is normally called poverty, and affects those living in conditions opposed to human dignity: those who lack basic rights and needs such as food, water, hygiene, work and the opportunity to develop and grow culturally. In response to this destitution, the Church offers her help...in meeting these needs and binding these wounds which disfigure the face of humanity. In the poor and outcast we see Christ's face; by loving and helping the poor, we love and serve Christ.

FRANCIS' LENTEN MESSAGE, 2014

SCRIPTURE

Rather, when you hold a banquet, invite the poor, the crippled, the lame, the blind; blessed indeed will you be because of their inability to repay you. For you will be repaid at the resurrection of the righteous.

LUKE 14:13–14

PRAYER

Dearest Lord, so often in our world people desire recompense for a good deed or to be repaid for assisting someone in need. I pray that my reward will not be of this earth. Instead I ask for the grace to seek out people in need without needing a reward. May I give generously to these people and see your face in theirs. May my prayers comfort them and may whatever I can offer them relieve their suffering to some extent. Amen.

LENTEN ACTION

In addition to offering your prayer in solidarity and your treasure to aid those throughout our world in greatest material need, spend some time exploring the efforts of a cause or organization you feel called to. Is there a way you can get involved with this organization in your community? If you aren't sure where to start, try researching Catholic Relief Services and see how you can get involved in some of their international ministries. Is there another way you can help work to abolish material destitution?

Day

14

Tuesday of the Second Week of Lent
Poor for Others

*L*ent is a fitting time for self-denial; we would do well to ask ourselves what we can give up in order to help and enrich others by our own poverty. Let us not forget that real poverty hurts: no self-denial is real without this dimension of penance. I distrust a charity that costs nothing and does not hurt.

FRANCIS' LENTEN MESSAGE, 2014

SCRIPTURE

> *Religion that is pure and undefiled before God and the Father is this: to care for orphans and widows in their affliction and to keep oneself unstained by the world.*

JAMES 1:27

PRAYER

Loving Lord Jesus Christ, you humbled yourself to live a life of poverty, offering solidarity to those who cried out for you, the true God. You returned to provide what was essential—the spirit of the law and to give us the greatest gift of all, your eternal friendship through your death and resurrection. Lord, use me as your willing instrument, that I might embrace the joy of the Gospel and exude its peace and elation to everyone I encounter, especially to anyone experiencing any kind of material, moral, or spiritual destitution. Amen.

LENTEN ACTION

In your journal, write down some of the ways you bear witness to the Good News of the Gospel in the way you live your life. How does your lifestyle model the poverty our Lord Jesus embraced? How does your speech, your thinking, what you eat, how you spend your money, and so on, reflect the manner in which the Gospel affects your life?

Spend time observing people you admire. How do these people bear witness to the Gospel in their daily lives? Write down a few of the examples they provide. Pray on these ways of bearing witness to the Gospel and let them sink in.

$\mathcal{D}$ay
15

Wednesday of the Second Week of Lent
Prayer Is Crucial

$\mathcal{P}$ rayer is the strength of the Christian and of every person who believes. In the weakness and frailty of our lives, we can turn to God with the confidence of children and enter into communion with him....Lent is a time of prayer, of more intense prayer, more prolonged, more assiduous, more able to take on the needs of the brethren; intercessory prayer, to intercede before God for the many situations of poverty and suffering.

FRANCIS' HOMILY AT HOLY MASS, BLESSING AND IMPOSITION
OF THE ASHES, BASILICA OF SANTA SABINA, MARCH 5, 2014

SCRIPTURE

Is anyone among you suffering? He should pray. Is anyone in good spirits? He should sing praise. Is anyone among you sick? He should summon the presbyters of the church, and they should pray over him and anoint [him] with oil in the name of the Lord, and the prayer of faith will save the sick person, and the Lord will raise him up. If he has committed any sins, he will be forgiven.

JAMES 5:13–15

PRAYER

Lord God, make every moment of my daily life a prayer to you. Grace me with the patience and endurance to keep you at the center of my life. Let me not simply reserve prayer with you for Sundays or before meals, but move me to offer up every act, every word, every thought, and every breath in praise of your name. May I also keep in mind those in greatest need in my parish community, city, country, and world. Help me make my life a prayer to you and keep you as my guiding light that aids me in navigating the ocean of life and illuminating those people who should be a priority. Amen.

LENTEN ACTION

There are many different styles of prayer available for every type of person and personality. Today, explore Centering Prayer. Allow ten to fifteen minutes for this practice.

Begin by sitting comfortably with your eyes closed. Choose a sacred word that best supports your sincere intention to be in the Lord's presence, such as "Jesus," "Lord," "God," "Savior," "Abba," "Divine," "Shalom," "Spirit," "Love," and so on. Let that word be gently present as the symbol of your sincere intention to be open to the Lord's divine action within you. (You can speak the word aloud or simply center on the thought of the word, leaving it unspoken.) Whenever you become aware of anything—thoughts, feelings, perceptions—return to your sacred word, your anchor. It is in this space God operates.

$\mathcal{D}$ay
16

Thursday of the Second Week of Lent
Our First Duty Is Prayer

$\mathcal{A}$ Church that is closed in on herself and in the past, a Church that only sees the little rules of behavior, of attitude, is a Church that betrays her own identity; a closed Church betrays her own identity! Then, let us rediscover today all the beauty and responsibility of being the Church apostolic! And remember this: the Church is apostolic because we pray—our first duty—and because we proclaim the Gospel by our life and by our words.

FRANCIS' GENERAL AUDIENCE, ST. PETER'S SQUARE, OCTOBER 16, 2013

SCRIPTURE

Rejoice in the Lord always. I shall say it again: rejoice! Your kindness should be known to all. The Lord is near. Have no anxiety at all, but in everything, by prayer and petition, with thanksgiving, make your requests known to God. Then the peace of God that surpasses all understanding will guard your hearts and minds in Christ Jesus.

PHILIPPIANS 4:4–7

Prayer

Lord God, our first duty to you as believers is prayer, and that makes perfect sense. The foundation of every strong relationship is good communication. Often when we pray we speak too much from our end, petitioning you for every little thing. Or the only time we pray is when we are in need of something. Yes, I do petition you, but with the caveat that what I ask is in accordance with your will. By knowing your will I better understand you and our friendship grows. I enjoy the quiet time when I can I hear your words, directing me to do your will. I thank you for this guidance because it leads me closer to you. Amen.

Lenten Action

Spend five to ten minutes reflecting on your prayer life. If the variety of your prayer time could be captured in a pie chart, what would it look like? Assign the appropriate sizes to the various types, or "slices," of prayer: rote prayer (Our Father, Hail Mary, rosary, Chaplet of Divine Mercy); casual dialogue; a monologue of prayers of petition; meditation on Scripture; Centering Prayer; other varieties of prayer (Eastern techniques, quiet time in the presence of the Blessed Sacrament); and anything else you incorporate into your prayer life. Is there anything you would like change about the balance of your prayer life? Is there anything you're not doing that you'd like to add or try?

$\mathcal{D}$ay
17

Friday of the Second Week of Lent
The Faith of Mary

*I*n the parable of the sower, St. Luke has left us these words of the Lord about the "good soil": "These are the ones who when they hear the word, hold it fast in an honest and good heart, and bear fruit with patient endurance" (Luke 8:15). In the context of Luke's Gospel, this mention of an honest and good heart which hears and keeps the word is an implicit portrayal of the faith of the Virgin Mary. The evangelist himself speaks of Mary's memory, how she treasured in her heart all that she had heard and seen, so that the word could bear fruit in her life.

FRANCIS' ENCYCLICAL LETTER *LUMEN FIDEI*, 58,
JUNE 29, 2013

Scripture

When Elizabeth heard Mary's greeting, the infant leaped in her womb, and Elizabeth, filled with the holy Spirit, cried out in a loud voice and said, "Most blessed are you among women, and blessed is the fruit of your womb....Blessed are you who believed that what was spoken to you by the Lord would be fulfilled."

LUKE 1:41–42, 45

Prayer

Blessed Virgin Mary, the humility you display is an inspiration to all believers. With you and St. Joseph raising our Lord and Savior, the essence of what it means to be a loving parent—that is, seeing to your child's needs from a physical, emotional, and spiritual point of view—is modeled right before our eyes on the pages of Scripture. We pray that you might intercede on behalf of all parents, dearest Mary, that they be graced with the passion and sense of gratitude and privilege to care for their children in the manner you exemplified. May they treasure the joys of their children and help their young ones to endure the inevitable suffering and sadness that life bears. May they be models of humility for their children, always open to God's will and divine plan. Amen.

Lenten Action

One of the tremendous graces we receive as believers is the opportunity to pray through Mary, our great intercessor. Obviously, Mary holds a special place in the plan of salvation but, from a mother-child perspective, she meant so much to Jesus during the period when she raised him. She was the impetus for his first public miracle at Cana; he would not refuse her request.

When was the last time you prayed to Jesus through Mary? Think of a current issue in your life or in the world and ask Mary to intercede for the sake of this issue's improvement or positive resolution. Echo some of the words of St. Elizabeth and close your prayer with a Hail Mary.

*D*ay

Saturday of the Second Week of Lent
Slavery to Sin

No less a concern is moral destitution, which consists in slavery to vice and sin. How much pain is caused in families because one of their members—often a young person—is in thrall to alcohol, drugs, gambling, or pornography! How many people no longer see meaning in life or prospects for the future, how many have lost hope!....This type of destitution, which also causes financial ruin, is invariably linked to the spiritual destitution which we experience when we turn away from God and reject his love.... God alone can truly save and free us.

Francis' Lenten Message, 2014

Scripture

No trial has come to you but what is human. God is faithful and will not let you be tried beyond your strength; but with the trial he will also provide a way out, so that you may be able to bear it.

1 Corinthians 10:13

PRAYER

Loving God, you provide a path of peace for us and never try us beyond our limits. We ask you to extend to us the virtue of prudence, that is, determining right from wrong in any given situation. We know that often situations are not as simple as one choice being good and the other evil. Prudence enables us to choose the greater of two goods in any given situation. We pray that you strengthen our resolve in these situations, that we always choose the greater good, that good which strengthens our relationship and deepens our intimacy with you. Amen.

LENTEN ACTION

Compose a prayer for someone (a person you know or an anonymous someone) who is a slave to vices and sin, elements of moral destitution elucidated by the Holy Father above, such as "alcohol, drugs, gambling, or pornography." Pray that this person finds substantial meaning in his or her life and that this meaning has its foundation rooted in God. Pray that this person is comforted by God's peace and the understanding that nothing is beyond his or her strength to overcome when God's grace is sought.

Day

19

Third Sunday of Lent
Spiritual Destitution

$\mathcal{T}$he Gospel is the real antidote to spiritual destitution: wherever we go, we are called as Christians to proclaim the liberating news that forgiveness for sins committed is possible, that God is greater than our sinfulness, that he freely loves us at all times and that we were made for communion and eternal life. The Lord asks us to be joyous heralds of this message of mercy and hope!....In union with Jesus, we can courageously open up new paths of evangelization and human promotion.

FRANCIS' LENTEN MESSAGE, 2014

SCRIPTURE

You know that he was revealed to take away sins, and in him there is no sin. No one who remains in him sins; no one who sins has seen him or known him. Children, let no one deceive you. The person who acts in righteousness is righteous, just as he is righteous.

1 JOHN 3:5–7

PRAYER

Dearest Father of promise and salvation, you sent your only Son to ransom us from that original sin that ended in death. The sin that seemed to forever separate the divine from its creation of man and woman was overcome by your generosity through Jesus Christ, bridging the gap between God and humanity like no other sacrifice in history. By this sacrifice, the sin of death was defeated and now we can be with you for all eternity. Death would not be the end; by participating in the salvation won by the death and resurrection of Jesus Christ, eternal life is ours. Our hope in you is not in vain; our hope in you allows for our eternal union and brings meaning to our daily lives. Amen.

LENTEN ACTION

Have you ever been at a place where you experienced the terror of spiritual desolation? This is a life lived without hope. There is no hope of meaning in your daily existence, no hope of life after death, no hope of a God that desires to love with boundless mercy. Perhaps you had been at this place in your life but you were rescued by the Gospel. Do you know a person who is experiencing spiritual desolation right now? He or she also can be rescued by the Gospel. Is there a way you can intervene and facilitate hope in the Gospel for this person during his or her suffering?

Day

20

Monday of the Third Week of Lent
Death Is a Gateway

*A*mong us there is commonly a mistaken way of looking at death. Death affects us all, and it questions us in a profound way, especially when it touches us closely, or when it takes the little ones, the defenseless in such a way that it seems "scandalous"....If it is understood as the end of everything, death frightens us, it terrifies us, it becomes a threat that shatters every dream, every promise, it severs every relationship and interrupts every journey. This happens when we consider our lives as a span of time between two poles: birth and death; when we fail to believe in a horizon that extends beyond that of the present life; when we live as though God did not exist.

FRANCIS' GENERAL AUDIENCE, ST. PETER'S SQUARE,
NOVEMBER 27, 2013

SCRIPTURE

This I declare, brothers: flesh and blood cannot inherit the kingdom of God, nor does corruption inherit incorruption. Behold, I tell you a mystery. We shall not all fall asleep, but we will all be changed, in an instant, in the blink of an eye, at the last trumpet. For the trumpet will sound, the dead will be raised incorruptible, and we shall be changed.

1 CORINTHIANS 15:50–52

PRAYER

Lord of eternal life, we know that death is not the end; we know that death is only the beginning of our everlasting life with you. We do not understand why terrible events occur—why people suffer through starvation, why people suffer through terminal illness, why children die—but as believers we trust that life has meaning, that God has a plan beyond our human comprehension. We have been graced with the gift of faith, and the more we trust in God the deeper our faith runs, the deeper our relationship with Jesus becomes. Lord, strengthen my faith, guide me where you will, and that will be enough for me. Amen.

LENTEN ACTION

When you read and hear about the suffering and death that takes place in the world, do you include any questions in your prayer to God as to why? When friends and loved ones are suffering, or when someone seems taken from your life too soon? How do you reconcile this in your relationship with the Lord? How does it affect your prayer? What do you say to God when you are angry or confused about suffering or perceived injustices in your own life? How do you respond when you are the one who is suffering? Is it an opportunity to grow deeper in faith and friendship with God? Take a few minutes and write your response in your journal.

$\mathcal{D}$ay
21

Tuesday of the Third Week of Lent
Suffering Aids Growth

To speak of faith often involves speaking of painful testing, yet it is precisely in such testing that Paul sees the most convincing proclamation of the Gospel, for it is in weakness and suffering that we discover God's power which triumphs over our weakness and suffering....Christians know that suffering cannot be eliminated, yet it can have meaning and become an act of love and entrustment into the hands of God who does not abandon us; in this way it can serve as a moment of growth in faith and love.

FRANCIS' ENCYCLICAL LETTER *LUMEN FIDEI*, 56, JUNE 29, 2013

SCRIPTURE

Beloved, do not be surprised that a trial by fire is occurring among you, as if something strange were happening to you. But rejoice to the extent that you share in the sufferings of Christ, so that when his glory is revealed you may also rejoice exultantly.

1 PETER 4:12–13

PRAYER

Lord God, there is much suffering in this world. All we have to do is watch the news. These reports of suffering surround us. We experience suffering in our personal lives as well. What to make of all of this? All I know is that without faith I would be lost in the midst of all this suffering. All meaning would be lost. If we are not awaiting something greater, it would be a struggle to find any semblance of meaning for the suffering we endure here. And yet, your Son sanctified everything he experienced, including suffering, so there is holiness to be found there as well. Help me grow closer to you in my own suffering this Lent. Thank you, God, and blessed be your name! Amen!

LENTEN ACTION

Recall an instance when you were suffering. Perhaps someone close to you was going through a very painful experience, emotionally or physically, and it tore you up to see him or her like this. Perhaps you were suffering, maybe from an excruciating medical procedure. How did this experience affect your relationship with God? Were you able to derive meaning from this pain and suffering, if only by reminding yourself that this mortal life is but a split second when compared to the eternity we are promised in the presence of our Lord and Savior? Did this comfort you? Did this negatively affect your relationship with God?

Day

22

Wednesday of the Third Week of Lent
God Draws Closer

Faith is not a light which scatters all our darkness, but a lamp which guides our steps in the night and suffices for the journey. To those who suffer, God does not provide arguments which explain everything; rather, his response is that of an accompanying presence, a history of goodness which touches every story of suffering and opens up a ray of light. In Christ, God himself wishes to share this path with us and to offer us his gaze so that we might see the light within it. Christ is the one who, having endured suffering, is "the pioneer and perfecter of our faith" (Hebrews 12:2).

FRANCIS' ENCYCLICAL LETTER *LUMEN FIDEI*, 57,
JUNE 29, 2013

Scripture

But we hold this treasure in earthen vessels, that the surpassing power may be of God and not from us. We are afflicted in every way, but not constrained; perplexed, but not driven to despair; persecuted, but not abandoned; struck down, but not destroyed; always carrying about in the body the dying of Jesus, so that the life of Jesus may also be manifested in our body.

2 Corinthians 4:7–10

Prayer

Heavenly Father, when I begin to concern myself with the "why" of suffering in this world it does me no good, nor does it benefit our relationship in the least. I find that when I pray that your will be done I am left with the source of faith that sustains our relationship on this earthly journey. Who am I to question your divine plan? You have given me the gift of faith that I might stand beside you through the good times and especially the bad. You are all good, you perfect my faith through trials and tribulations, suffering, and periods of loneliness. May I embrace these experiences for the opportunities they are. I ask this in the name of your Son, my Lord Jesus Christ.

LENTEN ACTION

Draw a time line of your spiritual life from your earliest memories of your relationship with God through today. Take ten to fifteen minutes to mark those moments on your time line when you felt closest to God. Try to fill in as many moments as you can. For those times when you regularly feel close to God (daily Mass, weekly reconciliation, an annual parish retreat, or other times), list those below your time line. Now review what you've written. Look at all those times in your life—happy or sad—when you felt the Lord journeying with you.

Day
23

Thursday of the Third Week of Lent
We Are the Dwelling Place of the Lord

*J*esus lived the daily reality of the most ordinary people: he was moved as he faced the crowd that seemed like a flock without a shepherd; he wept before the sorrow that Martha and Mary felt at the death of their brother, Lazarus; he called a publican to be his disciple; he also suffered betrayal by a friend. In him God has given us the certitude that he is with us, he is among us.

FRANCIS' GENERAL AUDIENCE, ST. PETER'S SQUARE,
MARCH 27, 2013

SCRIPTURE

Whoever acknowledges that Jesus is the Son of God, God remains in him and he in God. We have come to know and to believe in the love God has for us.

1 JOHN 4:15–16

Prayer

Loving God, you created us in your image and by becoming man through your Incarnation you sanctified our flesh. Thus, when we look into the face of one another we can see you dwelling within the other. How clear this makes our mission in life. To praise your name and serve you, we need only recognize your presence within our fellow brothers and sisters. When we see you in them, we can love you as we are called to, through service and prayer. Father, grace us with the ability to see you in everyone we meet and to respond in love through another. Amen.

Lenten Action

Set aside time for prayer tonight and early in the day tomorrow. Consider the fact that we are made in the image of God. As such, we are called to serve God by serving those within whom God dwells. Reflect on how you do this at present. Are you able to see the image and likeness of God in the faces of your fellow brothers and sisters? How do you respond when you encounter someone in need seeking your help? Pray that you see God in these people and respond as the need dictates.

Day
24

Friday of the Third Week of Lent
We Are Sons and Daughters of God

he eternal origin of Christ is in the Father. He is the Son in a total and unique sense, and so he is born in time without the intervention of a man. As the Son, Jesus brings to the world a new beginning and a new light, the fullness of God's faithful love bestowed on humanity....At the center of our faith is the confession of Jesus, the Son of God, born of a woman, who brings us, through the gift of the Holy Spirit, to adoption as sons and daughters (see Galatians 4:4).

FRANCIS' ENCYCLICAL LETTER *LUMEN FIDEI*, 59, JUNE 29, 2013

SCRIPTURE

[W]hen the fullness of time had come, God sent his Son, born of a woman, born under the law, to ransom those under the law, so that we might receive adoption. As proof that you are children, God sent the spirit of his Son into our hearts, crying out, "Abba, Father!" So you are no longer a slave but a child, and if a child then also an heir, through God.

GALATIANS 4:4–7

PRAYER

Jesus, you taught us to call our God "Father" and, as adopted sons and daughters, we share—to a lesser extent—in your divine sonship. You have called us your friends and we are your adopted brothers and sisters as well, under your one Father, imbued with the Spirit, and drawn into an intimacy with the divine Trinity. You do not seek praise and sacrifice as much as you seek fidelity and love. Grace us with the desire to provide this to your loving heart. Amen.

LENTEN ACTION

Consider how you—as a representative of your earthly family—represent your ancestors and your current family, including cousins and others. What stories do you tell? In what manner do you show them deference and respect? List the ways you respect your family's reputation by your behavior, by what you do and what you do not do. Consider now your Father in heaven, your adopted brother Jesus, the communion of saints, as well as your adopted brothers and sisters in the faith here on earth. List the ways you respect this spiritual family of faith.

$\mathcal{D}$ay

25

Saturday of the Third Week of Lent
Solidarity in God's Love

$\mathcal{W}$hat gives us true freedom, true salvation and true happiness is the compassion, tenderness and solidarity of [Christ's] love. Christ's poverty which enriches us is his taking flesh and bearing our weaknesses and sins as an expression of God's infinite mercy to us. Christ's poverty is the greatest treasure of all: Jesus' wealth is that of his boundless confidence in God the Father, his constant trust, his desire always and only to do the Father's will and give glory to him. Jesus is rich in the same way as a child who feels loved and who loves its parents, without doubting their love and tenderness for an instant.

FRANCIS' LENTEN MESSAGE, 2014

SCRIPTURE

[A] Samaritan traveler who came upon [the victim] was moved with compassion at the sight. He approached the victim, poured oil and wine over his wounds and bandaged them. Then he lifted him up on his own animal, took him to an inn and cared for him. The next day he took out two silver coins and gave them to the innkeeper with the instruction, 'Take care of him. If you spend more than what I have given you, I shall repay you on my way back.' Which of these three, in your opinion, was neighbor to the robbers' victim?" He answered, "The one who treated him with mercy." Jesus said to him, "Go and do likewise."

LUKE 10:33–37

PRAYER

Lord God, solidarity refers to the simple fact that we cannot live and exist well independent of others; we are interdependent beings. Solidarity looks upon this interdependence as something good, a thing to be cherished. The image St. Paul gives us of the body of Christ—that we are all individual parts making up the body of Christ—gives us a visual of this. You model solidarity for us through the Incarnation. What more can we do but ask for your grace to live our lives in the manner St. Paul describes and which you model? Amen.

Lenten Action

Take a few minutes to look up the definition of the word *solidarity*. Then in your journal respond to this: How does solidarity play a part in your life? Is it difficult for you to operate interdependently? Do you consider yourself a loner? How does functioning interdependently suit you? Is it challenging or does it come easily? How did your upbringing prepare you for operating in solidarity? Are you more comfortable with solidarity in a small group of like-minded people or can you see it in the worldwide Church?

Day
26

Fourth Sunday of Lent
Join the People of God

*W*hat does "People of God" mean? First of all it means that God does not belong in a special way to any one people; for it is He who calls us, convokes us, invites us to be part of his people, and this invitation is addressed to all, without distinction, for the mercy of God "desires all men to be saved" (1 Timothy 2:4)....I would also like to say to anyone who feels far away from God and the Church, to anyone who is timid or indifferent, to those who think they can no longer change: the Lord calls you too to become part in his people and he does this with great respect and love! He invites us to be part of this people, the People of God!

FRANCIS' GENERAL AUDIENCE, ST. PETER'S SQUARE,
JUNE 12, 2013

SCRIPTURE

For through faith you are all children of God in Christ Jesus.
For all of you who were baptized into Christ have clothed
yourselves with Christ. There is neither Jew nor Greek,
there is neither slave nor free person, there is not male and
female; for you are all one in Christ Jesus.

GALATIANS 3:26–28

PRAYER

Father of us all, as the People of God we are your Church, your children, your faithful. We accept your invitation to be a part of this beloved people. You love us so much you sacrificed your only Son so we might be with you for all eternity. You want everyone to be saved, not just an elite few. You ask that those of us who are your people go out to the four corners of the world and invite others, helping them to know your love by our words and—especially—by our actions. Enflame our hearts, dear Father, so that we go out and welcome all those who have not yet opened their hearts to you. We ask this in the name of your Son, our Lord Jesus Christ. Amen.

LENTEN ACTION

One day this week, attend Mass on a day other than Sunday. This could be a brief before-the-workday celebration of the Eucharist, a lunch-break Mass, or a lengthier evening gathering. During the sacrament of the Eucharist, be aware of the universality of the event. Every believer, every member of the People of God, every brother and sister of yours is celebrating the same Mass with you—it is truly universal! Whether you're in Rome or St. Louis, you are worshiping with your brothers and sisters. Reflect on that reality during the quieter moments of the Mass.

Day

27

Monday of the Fourth Week of Lent
The Kingdom of God

Ohat is the destination of this People? Our destination is the Kingdom of God, which God himself inaugurated on this earth and which must be extended until its fulfillment, when Christ, our life, shall appear (see *Lumen Gentium*, 9). The end then is full communion with the Lord, familiarity with the Lord, entry into his own divine life, where we will live in the joy of his love beyond measure, a full joy.

FRANCIS' GENERAL AUDIENCE, ST. PETER'S SQUARE,
JUNE 12, 2013

Scripture

He also said to them, "Amen, I say to you, there are some standing here who will not taste death until they see that the kingdom of God has come in power."

MARK 9:1

PRAYER

Mighty and loving God, king of kings, by your death and resurrection you won for us a victory over sin and death, and fulfilled the promise that we would be with you for all eternity in your heavenly kingdom. You also established on this earth the kingdom of God that we, as believers, are called to build up while we follow your will and the example modeled by your Son, our Lord Jesus. Grace us with your guidance, that our hearts remain open to your will, and that we participate in bringing the kingdom of God to its fulfillment on earth. Amen.

LENTEN ACTION

Participating in the kingdom of God here on earth means sharing the Good News of the Gospel, enjoying the nourishment of the Eucharist, establishing and maintaining friendships, praying on a regular basis, and many other activities encouraged by the Church. One activity that often gets neglected is the sacrament of reconciliation, the sacrament of forgiveness. It is an honest and trusting experience that cements a healthy relationship with our heavenly Father. Asking for and receiving God's forgiveness keeps us in a state of grace and in tune with the will of God. If you haven't experienced this sacrament in a while, consider going sometime soon.

Day
28

Tuesday of the Fourth Week of Lent
Foundation in Christ

Saint Paul writes to the Christians of Ephesus: "You are no longer strangers and sojourners, but you are fellow citizens with the saints and members of the household of God, built upon the foundation of the Apostles and prophets, Christ Jesus himself being a cornerstone" (2:19–20); that is, he compares Christians to living stones that form an edifice that is the Church, and this edifice is founded on the Apostles, like columns, and the cornerstone that carries it all is Jesus himself.

FRANCIS' GENERAL AUDIENCE, ST. PETER'S SQUARE,
OCTOBER 16, 2013

SCRIPTURE

> *So then you are no longer strangers and sojourners, but you are fellow citizens with the holy ones and members of the household of God, built upon the foundation of the apostles and prophets, with Christ Jesus himself as the capstone. Through him the whole structure is held together and grows into a temple sacred in the Lord; in him you also are being built together into a dwelling place of God in the Spirit.*

EPHESIANS 2:19–22

PRAYER

Lord Jesus, I read that you preached peace to those far off and those near, that through you we have access in one Spirit to the Father. The apostles continued this preaching in your name, reaching people far and wide, until there was almost no one who had not heard of your glory, your miracles, and your victory over sin and death. There are many believers like me, and that makes me happy; yet I am deeply saddened that even between believers there can be such division. We are called to be a foundation, but how can anything solid and lasting be built upon a foundation divided against itself? Help me, Lord, to promote unity. Amen.

LENTEN ACTION

Recall a time when you were at odds with someone. (Perhaps it is happening right now.) It could be a stranger, a neighbor, a family member, or someone you once considered to be a friend. What is at the heart of the division? Write it down. Study it. If Jesus has provided us access in one Spirit to the Father, how can a single issue divide one believer from another? How can our differences not be resolved? Write some options for resolution in your situation. Would a mediator benefit your cause? Or a letter that acknowledges hurt on both sides? Pray on this.

Day

29

Wednesday of the Fourth Week of Lent
Joseph Cared for Jesus

*J*oseph together with Mary, cared for Jesus above all from this point of view, that is he "raised" him, taking care that he lacked nothing he needed for healthy development....In those years Joseph instructed Jesus in his work, and Jesus learned to be a carpenter with his father Joseph. Thus Joseph raised Jesus.

FRANCIS' GENERAL AUDIENCE, ST. PETER'S SQUARE,
MARCH 19, 2014

SCRIPTURE

> *For the Lord sets a father in honor over his children*
> *and confirms a mother's authority over her sons.*
> *Those who honor their father atone for sins;*
> *they store up riches who respect their mother.*
> *Those who honor their father will have joy in their own*
> *children,*
> *and when they pray they are heard.*

SIRACH 3:2–5

PRAYER

Jesus, you honored your earthly stepfather and you honored your heavenly Father. As a child growing into a man, you learned from Joseph how to become a carpenter and what it meant to look after a family. You learned from your heavenly Father what it meant to be divine and what was entailed in your mission to suffer and die for the salvation of humanity. Lord, you knew from Joseph and Mary how fathers and mothers care so deeply for their offspring. Help us to appreciate the love of family as we continue through life's journey. Amen.

LENTEN ACTION

Look back on your formative years, growing up through childhood into your teenage years and into early adulthood. Who was your father figure? For many, our biological father showed us what it meant to lead and care for a family, what it meant to be responsible, to earn a living, and to make prudent decisions. Our parental figure taught us what it meant to worship, to respect others, and to love and honor our spouse. Reflect on that now. What kind of role model are you?

Day
30

Thursday of the Fourth Week of Lent
Our Father

ome of us have lost our dad, he has passed away, the Lord has called him; many in this square do not have their dad still with them. We can pray for all the fathers of the world, for the fathers living and deceased, as well as our own, and we can do it together, each one remembering his or her own father whether he be living or dead. And let us pray to the great Father of us all, the Father. An Our Father for our fathers.

FRANCIS' GENERAL AUDIENCE, ST. PETER'S SQUARE,
MARCH 19, 2014

"This is how you are to pray:
Our Father in heaven,
hallowed be your name,
your kingdom come,
your will be done,
on earth as in heaven.
Give us today our daily bread;
and forgive us our debts,
as we forgive our debtors;
and do not subject us to the final test,
but deliver us from the evil one."

MATTHEW 6:9–13

PRAYER

Heavenly Father, you who love us so dearly that you gave us your only Son for the sake of our salvation, words nor actions cannot express our gratitude for this overwhelming generosity. What we have received is pure grace, a true love from our Creator to us. May we be open to this grace and draw ever nearer to you, our Father, who we hope to share eternity with once we pass from this earth. We ask for your continued grace and praise you in all we say and do. Amen.

LENTEN ACTION

Write down each line of the Our Father, leaving five to six lines between each line of the prayer. Reflect on each line and then write whatever comes to your mind when you contemplate it. Make the written reflections personal: What does it mean to call God your Father? What does it mean to be given your daily bread? For which specific debts in your life do you seek forgiveness? What debtors are you called to forgive?

$\mathcal{D}$ay
31

Friday of the Fourth Week of Lent
We Are Not Islands

$\mathcal{T}$he Church and the Virgin Mary are mothers, both of them; what is said of the Church can be said also of Our Lady and what is said of Our Lady can also be said of the Church! Certainly faith is a personal act: "I believe," I personally respond to God who makes himself known and wants to enter into friendship with me (see *Lumen Fidei,* 39). But the faith I receive from others, within a family, within a community that teaches me to say "I believe," "we believe." A Christian is not an island!

FRANCIS' GENERAL AUDIENCE, ST. PETER'S SQUARE,
SEPTEMBER 11, 2013

SCRIPTURE

If the whole body were an eye, where would the hearing be? If the whole body were hearing, where would the sense of smell be? But as it is, God placed the parts, each one of them, in the body as he intended. If they were all one part, where would the body be? But as it is, there are many parts, yet one body.

1 CORINTHIANS 12:17–20

PRAYER

Great and loving God, I am blessed to have a personal, intimate relationship with you, but beyond that you have given me Mother Church as a community to nourish, encourage, and develop me. I am not meant to walk this earth in solitude, alone. I have been given family, friends, potential friends, and people to serve. I pray that you make my will your own, and I call upon the model of this servitude, the Blessed Virgin Mary, to intercede on my behalf in becoming a channel of your peace. I desire to build up your Church on this earth, and by serving the Church you love so dearly I grow closer to you. Amen.

LENTEN ACTION

Many of us spend a great deal of time on our own intimate relationship with Jesus, and this is a wonderful endeavor. What we sometimes lose sight of is the reality that Mother Church affords us the opportunity to grow even deeper in our relationship with Jesus. Jesus wants us to embrace the Church; he established it for our benefit. As a church we are called to mutually support each other, to lift each other up to the Lord. In your journal, write down two or three members of Mother Church who lift you up, who bring you closer to the Lord. How do they do it? How do you attempt to do this for others? How can you learn from the example of others?

Day

32

Saturday of the Fourth Week of Lent
The Church Is With Us

*I*n a word, a good mother helps her children to come of themselves, and not to remain comfortably under her motherly wings, like a brood of chicks under the wings of the broody hen. The Church, like a good mother, does the same thing: she accompanies our development by transmitting to us the Word of God, which is a light that directs the path of Christian life; she administers the Sacraments. She nourishes us with the Eucharist, she brings us the forgiveness of God through the Sacrament of Penance, she helps us in moments of sickness with the Anointing of the sick. The Church accompanies us throughout our entire life of faith, throughout the whole of our Christian life.

FRANCIS' GENERAL AUDIENCE, ST. PETER'S SQUARE,
SEPTEMBER 11, 2013

SCRIPTURE

[W]hat we have seen and heard we proclaim now to you, so that you too may have fellowship with us; for our fellowship is with the Father and with his Son, Jesus Christ. We are writing this so that our joy may be complete.

1 JOHN 1:3–4

PRAYER

Lord God, you gave us the Church for our spiritual benefit; we do not participate alone in the salvation won by Christ. We unite in communion with our fellow believers, our brothers and sisters in Christ on our earthly journey. We are called to be there for one another in our times of need. Together we raise each other up when another stumbles, we model your love for the edification of our brothers and sisters in Christ. Grace us, dear Lord, with the compassion and courage to embrace your Church and throw ourselves completely into it. Guide us, loving Lord, and we will follow your will. Amen.

LENTEN ACTION

What is your current relationship with the Church? Journal your answer to this question for ten minutes and reflect on how you have responded. If your relationship with the Church is formal or awkward, or you would like to see it deepened, have you considered speaking with someone in your local parish church about what steps you can take to strengthen this relationship?

$\mathcal{D}$ay

33

Fifth Sunday of Lent
Carry the Light of the Gospel

What is this people's mission? It is to bring the hope and salvation of God to the world: to be a sign of the love of God who calls everyone to friendship with Him; to be the leaven that makes the dough rise, the salt that gives flavor and preserves from corruption, to be a light that enlightens....Let our lives together be the one light of Christ; together we will carry the light of the Gospel to the whole of reality.

FRANCIS' GENERAL AUDIENCE, ST. PETER'S SQUARE,
JUNE 12, 2013

SCRIPTURE

Indeed, the word of God is living and effective, sharper than any two-edged sword, penetrating even between soul and spirit, joints and marrow, and able to discern reflections and thoughts of the heart.

HEBREWS 4:12

PRAYER

Lord God, there are some days when—after I read the newspaper or listen to the radio—I feel the world is getting worse and evil is winning. I must remind myself that your Son, our Lord Jesus, has already conquered sin and death, that victory has been won for humanity through his sacrifice on the cross and his resurrection on the Sunday called Easter. We are called not to dwell on the evils that people perpetrate throughout the world but to participate in the salvation that has been won on our behalf. Lord, center my heart on what is good and holy. Let me focus on the good I can do and not worry about what is beyond my control. Amen.

LENTEN ACTION

Do you ever feel down when you read or watch the local, national, or international news? Take a break from the news for a day or two and only focus on good news or inspirational stories. Good things happen all the time; they just don't get reported like the bad news. Take ten minutes and journal the titles of some books or films you know will lift your spirit. Make time to read sections of these books and watch a few of these films. Surf the internet for positive stories happening in our world right now. Lift your spirit for the Spirit that wants you to be aflame with the Good News and share it with your neighbors, your friends, your family, and the world.

$\mathcal{D}$ay
34

Monday of the Fifth Week of Lent
Pray and Proclaim the Gospel

*T*o profess that the Church is apostolic means to stress the constitutive bond that she has with the Apostles, with that small group of twelve men whom Jesus one day called to himself, he called them by name, that they might remain with him and that he might send them out to preach (see Mark 3:13–19). An Apostle is a person who has been given a mandate, he is sent to do something and the Apostles were chosen, called and sent out by Jesus to continue his work.

FRANCIS' GENERAL AUDIENCE, ST. PETER'S SQUARE,
OCTOBER 16, 2013

SCRIPTURE

He went up the mountain and summoned those whom he wanted and they came to him. He appointed twelve [whom he also named apostles] that they might be with him and he might send them forth to preach and to have authority to drive out demons.

MARK 3:13–15

PRAYER

Loving Lord Jesus, just as you chose the Twelve Apostles during your earthly ministry, so also have you chosen me as your friend and follower. When I pray I can hear you and feel you call my name, saying, "Come, follow me." How can I refuse? How can I say no to such an invitation of love, freedom, peace, and joy? I cannot. You call and I come. You ask that I pray; this is my pleasure. You ask that I proclaim your Gospel; this is my pleasure as well. Continue your calling, Lord Jesus, that I may hear your voice and follow you to eternal life. Amen.

LENTEN ACTION

In your journal, reply to this: As a follower of Jesus, how do you "continue his work, that is to pray...and...proclaim the Gospel?" How has your prayer life evolved as you've grown in your faith? Have you always been a good prayer listener or has that taken a disciplined approach? Did you begin with rote prayers and move into different styles of prayer? As for preaching the Gospel, how has that developed throughout your life? Is it a combination of words and actions? How have you developed confidence in proclaiming the Gospel?

Day

35

Tuesday of the Fifth Week of Lent
Pass on the Faith

*H*ow could what the Apostles experienced with Jesus, what they heard from him, reach us? This is the second meaning of the term "apostolic." ...Over the centuries, the Church conserves this precious treasure, which is Sacred Scripture, doctrine, the Sacraments, the ministry of Pastors, so that we can be faithful to Christ and share in his very life. It is like a river coursing through history, developing, irrigating; but running water always comes from a source, and the source is Christ himself.

FRANCIS' GENERAL AUDIENCE, ST. PETER'S SQUARE,
OCTOBER 16, 2013

SCRIPTURE

*But we ought to give thanks to God for you always, brothers
loved by the Lord, because God chose you as the firstfruits
for salvation through sanctification by the Spirit and belief
in truth. To this end he has [also] called you through our
gospel to possess the glory of our Lord Jesus Christ. Therefore,
brothers, stand firm and hold fast to the traditions that you
were taught, either by an oral statement or by a letter of
ours.*

2 THESSALONIANS 2:13–15

PRAYER

Loving Lord, Word made flesh through the mystery of the
Incarnation, you were sent by the Father to redeem us all—
the greatest story ever told! It is such a great story it seems
too good to be true, but its greatness lies in the fact that it is
as true today as it was 2,000 years ago. We are called to pass
on this story with joy in our hearts to our own generation
and the generation that follows us. May my loving actions
spread your Gospel as you have instructed me. I ask this in
your name, my Lord Jesus. Amen.

LENTEN ACTION

Jesus has given us the gift to spread his Good News. Are we aware that we have that gift? Preaching usually doesn't make it to the top of people's "Favorite Things to Do" lists, but there are many other ways to spread the Good News. So follow the Church. Communicate what the Church teaches. Reflect on this and write three to five Church teachings that you would like to pass along to the next generation of believers. How will you spread this Good News and to whom would you like to reach out?

$\mathcal{D}$ay
36

Wednesday of the Fifth Week of Lent
Joy of the Gospel

$\mathcal{T}$he Church continues in history the mission which Jesus entrusted to the Apostles: "Go therefore and make disciples of all nations, baptizing them in the name of the Father and of the Son and of the Holy Spirit, teaching them to observe all that I have commanded you; and lo, I am with you always, to the close of the age" (Matthew 28:19–20). This is what Jesus told us to do! I insist on this missionary aspect, because Christ invites all to "go out" and encounter others, he sends us, he asks us to move in order to spread the joy of the Gospel!

FRANCIS' GENERAL AUDIENCE, ST. PETER'S SQUARE,
OCTOBER 16, 2013

SCRIPTURE

Remain in me, as I remain in you. Just as a branch cannot bear fruit on its own unless it remains on the vine, so neither can you unless you remain in me. I am the vine, you are the branches. Whoever remains in me and I in him will bear much fruit, because without me you can do nothing.

JOHN 15:4–5

PRAYER

Loving Jesus, it is only through you that I am able to do anything. Any talent I have is a gift from you, any inclination to do good is inspired by your grace—my life itself is a gift from you! Your love is my love, and I am called to be a missionary to the world. I am a missionary to my children who live down the hall, to my neighbor fifty feet from my front door, to a person from Israel I might sit next to at the airport. Use me as you will, I am your instrument, a member of your Church. I love you more than words—allow me to show you when I see your image in the face of another. Amen.

LENTEN ACTION

Think on the following questions for a few minutes tonight or when you wake tomorrow morning. Pray on them as well, and unite your desire with that of the Holy Father's to break outside of your self-imposed restrictions and embrace God's call. Are you a missionary by words? By your actions? Have you confined your faith to Sundays only? Or is faith part of your life every day? What kind of Christian are you?

Day

37

Thursday of the Fifth Week of Lent
Joseph Modeled Grace

*J*oseph's mission is certainly unique and unrepeatable, because Jesus is absolutely unique. And yet, in his guardianship of Jesus, forming him to grow in age, wisdom and grace, he is a model for every educator, especially every father. Saint Joseph is the model of the educator and the dad, the father.

FRANCIS' GENERAL AUDIENCE, ST. PETER'S SQUARE,
MARCH 19, 2014

SCRIPTURE

For by grace you have been saved through faith, and this is not from you; it is the gift of God; it is not from works, so no one may boast.

EPHESIANS 2:8–9

82

Prayer

Lord Jesus, you modeled for us what it means to be perfect and sinless, a goal to strive for despite the fact our human failings cause us to fall short. When I fall down, lift me up. Lord, I ask this day for the grace to persevere in my faith in my words and in my actions. Move me to be an instrument of your peace. Grace me that I might educate and lead others to the grace and peace I experience with you. May my example inspire others to seek you out in their own lives. Amen.

Lenten Action

How blessed Joseph was to be married to Mary and to serve as the stepfather of the Savior of humanity. We can only assume he accepted these graces with the same humility and joy that he exemplifies during those few times he is mentioned in Scripture.

In today's journal, list the wonderful graces God has given you throughout your life. Be specific in your list, don't just list the name of a friend as a grace from God in your life; expand as to why this friend is a grace (that is, what unique and special blessings does he or she bring to your daily life?). Give this exercise as much time as it takes.

Day

38

Friday of the Fifth Week of Lent
Called to Evangelize

*I*n the first centuries of the Church, one thing was very clear: the Church, while being the mother of Christians, while "making" Christians, is also "made" by them. The Church is not distinct from us, but should be seen as the totality of believers, as the "we" of Christians: I, you, we all are part of the Church.

FRANCIS' GENERAL AUDIENCE, ST. PETER'S SQUARE,
SEPTEMBER 11, 2013

SCRIPTURE

You are the light of the world. A city set on a mountain
cannot be hidden. Nor do they light a lamp and then put
it under a bushel basket; it is set on a lampstand, where it
gives light to all in the house. Just so, your light must shine
before others, that they may see your good deeds and glorify
your heavenly Father.

MATTHEW 5:14–16

Prayer

Lord Jesus, the call to evangelize can be an intimidating prospect; it calls to mind the great evangelizers of the Church's history, many of whom were unwelcomed and martyred for the faith. It still happens today. Most of us are not called to travel to distant lands to preach your saving Gospel, but the prospect of speaking about our faith or defending our beliefs can be frightening. We have our Bible and our *Catechism*, but most of all we have our Christian actions, modeled after your own when you walked this earth 2,000 years ago. With all of this, there is no place for fear. Amen.

Lenten Action

Reflect on today's words from Pope Francis. What is your role in the Church? How are you living it? How are you helping others in their roles?

$\mathcal{D}ay$

39

Saturday of the Fifth Week of Lent
The Law of Love

*W*hat is the law of the People of God? It is the law of love, love for God and love for neighbor according to the new commandment that the Lord left to us (see John 13:34). It is a love, however, that is not sterile sentimentality or something vague, but the acknowledgment of God as the one Lord of life and, at the same time, the acceptance of the other as my true brother, overcoming division, rivalry, misunderstanding, selfishness; these two things go together....To pray for those with whom we are angry is a beautiful step towards that law of love.

Francis' General Audience, St. Peter's Square,
June 12, 2013

Scripture

I give you a new commandment: love one another. As I have loved you, so you also should love one another. This is how all will know that you are my disciples, if you have love for one another.

John 13:34–35

Prayer

Grand and loving God, while we love you we are sometimes confounded as to how to display that love for you. Years ago, believers would offer you a sacrifice or the "firstfruits" of their harvest—material things you have no use for. You do not desire sacrifice; you desire righteousness and you desire our love. But how? We must recall that we are made in your image, that you abide in us. If we cannot see you in another, then we have failed to love you. We must love you by serving you through our neighbor, who we must love like ourselves. We pray that you grace us with this disposition. Amen.

Lenten Action

How do you love yourself? If you're not taking care of yourself, respecting yourself—eating well, getting enough sleep, exercising, praying, engaging in life-affirming work or hobbies, reading spiritually fulfilling books—your critical self-love will carry over to love of neighbor accordingly. So love yourself. Take time for yourself. Forgive yourself. Treat yourself well. Use positive self talk. This will benefit you greatly in following the second-greatest commandment.

Day
40

Palm Sunday
Open Our Hearts

*H*oly Week is a time of grace which the Lord gives us to open the doors of our heart, of our life, of our parishes—what a pity so many parishes are closed!—of the movements, of the associations; and "to come out" in order to meet others, to make ourselves close, to bring them the light and joy of our faith.

Francis' General Audience, St. Peter's Square,
March 27, 2013

Scripture

I charge you in the presence of God and of Christ Jesus, who will judge the living and the dead, and by his appearing and his kingly power: proclaim the word; be persistent whether it is convenient or inconvenient; convince, reprimand, encourage through all patience and teaching. For the time will come when people will not tolerate sound doctrine but, following their own desires and insatiable curiosity, will accumulate teachers and will stop listening to the truth and will be diverted to myths.

2 Timothy 4:1–4

PRAYER

Lord God, heavenly Father, I open my heart to you. As we begin this Holy Week, I pray that an outpouring of your grace fills my heart and that the joy and peace I have inside shines like a beacon to those around me. May they experience you through their encounter with me. You have made your promise to me, dear Lord; may I make a promise to you: that I open my heart as a willing vessel of your divine plan. Let all who see me, hear me, and observe me know that I am guided by you. Amen.

LENTEN ACTION

Write a note (or an email) to someone close to you who has been dealing with a family member's illness, his own physical or emotional pain, the loss of a job, depression, or other issues. Let him know you're thinking of him during this time, and that you've devoted this Holy Week to praying for him. Pray for him every day and remind him that he is not alone. God is present with him; he is in your thoughts and prayers. Commit five to ten minutes of prayer to this person each day of this Holy Week.

Day

41

Monday of Holy Week
Everything Great About God

What does living Holy Week mean to us? What does following Jesus on his journey to Calvary on his way to the Cross and the Resurrection mean? In his earthly mission Jesus walked the roads of the Holy Land; he called 12 simple people to stay with him, to share his journey and to continue his mission. He chose them from among the people full of faith in God's promises. He spoke to all without distinction: the great and the lowly, the rich young man and the poor widow, the powerful and the weak; he brought God's mercy and forgiveness; he healed, he comforted, he understood; he gave hope.

FRANCIS' GENERAL AUDIENCE, ST. PETER'S SQUARE,
MARCH 27, 2013

SCRIPTURE

> ...*God, who is rich in mercy, because of the great love he had*
> *for us, even when we were dead in our transgressions, brought*
> *us to life with Christ (by grace you have been saved).*

EPHESIANS 2:4–5

PRAYER

Jesus, my dearest friend, every wonderful, loving facet of the divine you put on display for us. In the flesh, you brought these divine aspects to a world thirsting for such beauty, such life-giving qualities. To make it all the more special, you sanctified our flesh with these divine qualities. We may not be able to work miracles in the same manner that you did, but we can participate in healing others, comforting our brothers and sisters, understanding people who feel alone, giving hope to those in despair, and caring for those in greatest need. Thank you, Lord Jesus, for imparting these divine qualities to your creation, that we might share in them and become closer to one another and to you. Amen.

LENTEN ACTION

Of the divine qualities listed by the Holy Father above, which do you feel most graced with in your daily life? Are you a healer of division (or of pain)? Is your specialty comforting those in sorrow? Do you excel in lending an ear for the sake of understanding? Do you provide hope, encouragement, and support for those who need them desperately? How did God help you develop these qualities throughout your life?

Day

42

Tuesday of Holy Week
For Love of Us

*J*esus gives himself without reserve, he keeps nothing for himself, not even life. At the Last Supper, with his friends, he breaks the bread and passes the cup round "for us." The Son of God offers himself to us, he puts his Body and his Blood into our hands, so as to be with us always, to dwell among us.

FRANCIS' GENERAL AUDIENCE, ST. PETER'S SQUARE,
MARCH 27, 2013

SCRIPTURE

> *Yet it was our pain that he bore,*
> *our sufferings he endured.*
> *We thought of him as stricken,*
> *struck down by God and afflicted,*
> *But he was pierced for our sins,*
> *crushed for our iniquity.*
> *He bore the punishment that makes us whole,*
> *by his wounds we were healed.*

ISAIAH 53:4–5

Prayer

Heavenly Father, we thank you for the gift of your Son, our Lord Jesus Christ. For our Creator to become one of us, to live among us, to teach us, to suffer and die so that we might be able to enjoy your presence for all eternity—this is indeed the greatest gift in the history of the world. Jesus kept nothing for himself, he held nothing back, and gave his own life for our sake. How deep is that love? We can only imagine. Our human limitations leave us guessing. We are left with only our gratitude. Thank you. Amen.

Lenten Action

It can be overwhelming to try to understand the depth of love involved in the mystery of the Incarnation and the fact that God loves us so much he became man, lived among us, suffered and died for our sins, and defeated death on our behalf so we might gain eternal life. We could not ask for a greater gift.

To put the depth of love that surrounds God's gift to us in perspective, write in your journal about the greatest gift you've ever received from another person. What made this gift so special? Do you still have it? Was it something tangible, concrete, or a gift that was not a material thing?

Day

43

Wednesday of Holy Week
Life Does Not End With Death

*I*f we look at the most painful moments of our lives, when we have lost a loved one—our parents, a brother, a sister, a spouse, a child, a friend—we realize that even amid the tragedy of loss, even when torn by separation, the conviction arises in the heart that everything cannot be over, that the good given and received has not been pointless. There is a powerful instinct within us which tells us that our lives do not end with death.

FRANCIS' GENERAL AUDIENCE, ST. PETER'S SQUARE,
NOVEMBER 27, 2013

SCRIPTURE

For if we believe that Jesus died and rose, so too will God, through Jesus, bring with him those who have fallen asleep. Indeed, we tell you this, on the word of the Lord, that we who are alive, who are left until the coming of the Lord, will surely not precede those who have fallen asleep.

1 THESSALONIANS 4:14–15

PRAYER

Lord Jesus, you defeated death and won for us eternal salvation. Sometimes when we dwell on the subject of death, we tie ourselves up in knots of anxiety and dread. Yes, death can be a frightening and saddening prospect. We know not know when it comes; it is often preceded by pain and suffering. And when we lose someone close to us, the emotional pain, the grief, can feel like it is too much to bear. But in our hearts we know this transition from life into death into an afterlife with you is but an instant. We must keep this knowledge in our minds and our hearts. Your grace and consolation can aid us in overcoming any fear. Amen.

LENTEN ACTION

Holy Week centers on the death of Jesus on Good Friday. It is a solemn week, to say the least. It is a week that, were it not for the end we know is coming, would be filled with tremendous despair. If Holy Week ended only in death, what would it all have meant? Where would we be? But there is more, and that knowledge is already inside of us. Spend the next ten to fifteen minutes reflecting on the promise made throughout Scripture. You know it in your heart. Death is not the end. Why is this knowledge present inside of you? Where does this powerful instinct come from?

Day

44

Holy Thursday
Share Your Faith

*I*n the acts of the martyrs, we read the following dialogue between the Roman prefect Rusticus and a Christian named Hierax: "'Where are your parents?' the judge asked the martyr. He replied: 'Our true father is Christ, and our mother is faith in him.'" For those early Christians, faith, as an encounter with the living God revealed in Christ, was indeed a "mother," for it had brought them to the light and given birth within them to divine life, a new experience and a luminous vision of existence for which they were prepared to bear public witness to the end.

FRANCIS' ENCYCLICAL LETTER *LUMEN FIDEI*, 5, JUNE 29, 2013

SCRIPTURE

Simon, Simon, behold Satan has demanded to sift all of you like wheat, but I have prayed that your own faith may not fail; and once you have turned back, you must strengthen your brothers.

LUKE 22:31–32

PRAYER

Lord Jesus, even with your prayer supporting the strength of his conviction, Peter was overcome by fear and denied knowing you three times. Peter had every intention of going to prison and dying with you, but still his faith failed. We try, Lord; no one knows that better or to a greater depth than you. We fall and we get up. We stumble and you help us to our feet time and again. With such love in our favor, how can we fail? Continue to pray for us as you did with Peter, and we will continue to try to publicly proclaim our faith in you despite any threat of mocking, retribution, violence, or death. Amen.

LENTEN ACTION

Bearing public witness to one's faith can be an intimidating prospect. If we fail to bear witness in the manner we are called, let us not despair, for Christ is still with us. Spend five to ten minutes journaling on a time when you chose silence over public witness because of fear or embarrassment. Try not to feel shame; instead take comfort in the fact that you shared a common moment of weakness with at least one great saint.

Day

45

Good Friday
The Height of Human Suffering

As we contemplate Jesus in his Passion, we see reflected the suffering of humanity, and we discover the divine answer to the mystery of evil, suffering, and death. Many times we feel horror at the evil and suffering that surrounds us and we ask ourselves: "Why does God allow it?"....And Jesus takes all of this evil, all of this suffering upon himself. This week it would benefit all of us to look at the crucifix, to kiss the wounds of Jesus, to kiss them on the crucifix. He took upon himself all human suffering, he clothed himself in this suffering.

FRANCIS' GENERAL AUDIENCE, ST. PETER'S SQUARE,
APRIL 16, 2014

SCRIPTURE

Those passing by reviled him, shaking their heads and saying, "You who would destroy the temple and rebuild it in three days, save yourself, if you are the Son of God, [and] come down from the cross!" Likewise the chief priests with the scribes and elders mocked him and said, "He saved others; he cannot save himself. So he is the king of Israel! Let him come down from the cross now, and we will believe in him."

MATTHEW 27:39–42

PRAYER

All-loving Lord who died on the cross for our sins, you took all the evil, suffering, and death upon yourself, everything that frightens us in this world, you embraced it with your humanity, and you defeated it with your divinity. This act of selfless love bridged the chasm between the human and the divine begun by Adam's sin and carried throughout human history. It reached its completion when you rose on the third day, as you predicted. Any suffering I experience in my life, dear Jesus, I offer up in kinship with the suffering you went through during the scourging at the pillar, the crowning with thorns, your painful road to Calvary, and the excruciating hours you spent upon the cross until your dying breath. Amen.

Lenten Action

Go to your local church and contemplate the Stations of the Cross. Most churches have these stations lining their interior walls. During the Fridays of Lent, many churches offer a Stations of the Cross prayer service as well; but even if this is not offered at your church, or you cannot make the scheduled service, you can move from station to station, contemplating and experiencing in prayer the suffering experienced by Jesus on the day of his death.

$\mathcal{D}$ay
46

Holy Saturday
Without Hope, Faith Is Incomplete

*S*uffering reminds us that faith's service to the common good is always one of hope—a hope which looks ever ahead in the knowledge that only from God, from the future which comes from the risen Jesus, can our society find solid and lasting foundations. In this sense faith is linked to hope, for even if our dwelling place here below is wasting away, we have an eternal dwelling place which God has already prepared in Christ, in his body (see 2 Corinthians 4:16—5:5).

FRANCIS' ENCYCLICAL LETTER *LUMEN FIDEI*, 57,
JUNE 29, 2013

SCRIPTURE

Let what you heard from the beginning remain in you. If what you heard from the beginning remains in you, then you will remain in the Son and in the Father. And this is the promise that he made us: eternal life.

1 JOHN 2:24–25

PRAYER

God my Father, there are times when hope is so rooted in my faith that I cannot tell the difference between the two—they seem one and the same. My faith in you is my hope of intimate friendship with you; my faith in you is my hope that I am serving your will; my faith in you is my hope of spending my eternal life in your blessed presence. What would faith be if it were not rooted in hope? My faith in you is my hope in your promise of my future. My faith directs my purpose and my daily life according to your will. My hope is all in you. Amen.

LENTEN ACTION

In today's journal, write about the hopes you had as a child. You may have hoped to be invited to a birthday party, to see a special present under the tree on Christmas morning, or hoped not to get a certain teacher for fourth grade. Then, write about your hopes at the present time. Are they more faith-based than those listed in the first paragraph? What do these hopes center on? Do you envision these hopes changing in the years to come?

PART II

~~~

READINGS *for* EASTER

*D*ay
47

Easter
The Eucharist Is Our Nourishment

*T*he sacramental character of faith finds its highest expression in the Eucharist. The Eucharist is a precious nourishment for faith: an encounter with Christ truly present in the supreme act of his love, the life-giving gift of himself. In the Eucharist we find the intersection of faith's two dimensions....In the Eucharist we learn to see the heights and depths of reality. The bread and wine are changed into the body and blood of Christ, who becomes present in his passover to the Father: this movement draws us, body and soul, into the movement of all creation towards its fulfilment in God.

FRANCIS' ENCYCLICAL LETTER *LUMEN FIDEI*, 44, JUNE 29, 2013

SCRIPTURE

So also is the resurrection of the dead. It is sown corruptible;
it is raised incorruptible. It is sown dishonorable; it is raised
glorious. It is sown weak; it is raised powerful. It is sown
a natural body; it is raised a spiritual body. If there is a
natural body, there is also a spiritual one.

1 CORINTHIANS 15:42–44

PRAYER

Hallelujah! Today is the feast of the Resurrection, the final movement in the symphony of salvation has been played. The last transformation from the earthly to the spiritual has been completed in our Lord's victory over death. What once separated us from the divine has been restored by the Lamb of God. Today is a day of rebirth, of unity restored, of communion, and of celebration. It was a new day then, nearly 2,000 years ago, and it has been a new day on every Easter since. Let us give praise for this reunion and cherish the face of Christ in everyone we encounter. Amen! Amen!

EASTER ACTION

Today is a day of joyous celebration. When you attend Easter Mass, be present to the Lord as best you can. Put all worry and distraction out of your mind; focus on each part of the Mass—be in the present moment during the music and singing, the scriptural readings, the homily, the general intercessions, the Eucharistic Prayer, during Communion, and through the dismissal and recessional hymn. This is a day to celebrate with the Lord and his creation, your brothers and sisters in faith. Be joyful and at peace as the Lord desires you to be. Express your love for the Lord today in the manner he calls you to.

Day

48

Easter Monday
We Celebrate the Resurrection

"Why do you seek the living among the dead?" (Luke 24:5).

hese words are like a milestone in history; but are also like a "stumbling block" if we do not open ourselves to the Good News, if we think that a dead Jesus is less bothersome than a Jesus who is alive! Yet how many times along our daily journey do we need to hear it said: "Why do you seek the living among the dead?" How often do we search for life among inert things, among things that cannot give life, among things that are here today and gone tomorrow, among the things that pass away?

FRANCIS' GENERAL AUDIENCE, ST. PETER'S SQUARE,
APRIL 23, 2014

SCRIPTURE

They said to them, "Why do you seek the living one among the dead? He is not here, but he has been raised. Remember what he said to you while he was still in Galilee, that the Son of Man must be handed over to sinners and be crucified, and rise on the third day." And they remembered his words. Then they returned from the tomb and announced all these things to the eleven and to all the others.

LUKE 24:5–9

PRAYER

Loving Jesus, how often do I seek the living among the dead in the activities I pursue and the time I give to certain distractions? I confess that I do these things too much in my daily life, wasting the time you have given me on this earth to grow closer to you in friendship and strengthen those relationships in my life that help me to better know your love. Grace me, I pray, with the prudence to choose wisely how I spend my time. I pray that I pay close attention to what I read, watch, say, think, with whom I spend my time, and what I spend my time doing. In all these things may I be alert enough to ask whether or not what I am doing is bringing me closer to you. Amen.

EASTER ACTION

Regardless of how much free time you have, make a list of the different ways you spend your leisure time. If you like to read books, list the titles of those books; do the same with the television shows and movies you watch. Then review the list, item by item, and ask yourself this question after each item: "How does this activity bring me closer to God?" Hopefully, this exercise will give you a clearer perspective of how you pursue a deeper intimacy with God during your free time.

Day
49

Easter Tuesday
Mary Is Mother of All

*M*ary's true motherhood also ensured for the Son of God an authentic human history, true flesh in which he would die on the cross and rise from the dead. Mary would accompany Jesus to the cross (see John 19:25), whence her motherhood would extend to each of his disciples (see John 19:26–27). She will also be present in the upper room after Jesus' resurrection and ascension, joining the Apostles in imploring the gift of the Spirit (see Acts 1:14).

FRANCIS' ENCYCLICAL LETTER *LUMEN FIDEI*, 59,
JUNE 29, 2013

SCRIPTURE

When Jesus saw his mother and the disciple there whom he loved, he said to his mother, "Woman, behold, your son." Then he said to the disciple, "Behold, your mother." And from that hour the disciple took her into his home.

JOHN 19:26–27

PRAYER

Blessed Virgin, we come to you as our great intercessor, since we know your Son cannot refuse you. When he became incarnate through that wonderful mystery that united God and man, you provided the humanity that allowed for our acceptance as adoptive brothers and sisters in Christ. This was only possible through the humanity you provided as his mother, conceived without sin. Keep us close to your heart; you are our spiritual mother, guiding us, teaching us, nurturing us. Amen.

EASTER ACTION

Write each line of the Hail Mary prayer, leaving at least five to six lines between each line/phrase of the prayer. Reflect on each line and then write whatever comes to your mind when you contemplate that line of the prayer. Make the written reflections personal. Complete this exercise by saying the Hail Mary slowly, deliberately, keeping in mind those reflections you wrote following each line/phrase.

Day

50

Easter Wednesday
Our Resurrection

oday I wish to return to the affirmation "I believe in the resurrection of the body." This is not a simple truth and it is anything but obvious; living immersed in this world it is not easy for us to fathom a future reality. But the Gospel enlightens us: our resurrection is strictly bound to Jesus' resurrection. The fact that he is risen is the proof that there is a resurrection of the dead.

FRANCIS' GENERAL AUDIENCE, ST. PETER'S SQUARE,
DECEMBER 4, 2013

SCRIPTURE

[A]re you unaware that we who were baptized into Christ Jesus were baptized into his death? We were indeed buried with him through baptism into death, so that, just as Christ was raised from the dead by the glory of the Father, we too might live in newness of life.

ROMANS 6:3–4

PRAYER

Lord Jesus, on Holy Thursday during the Last Supper, you shared a meal with your apostles, saying, "This is my body, which will be given for you; do this in memory of me" (Luke 22:19). What you gave to them, and what you give to us at each Eucharist, is the Bread of Life. You are the Bread of Life. We believers who eat your body and drink your blood are nourished by the sustenance of salvation. Your risen body, your resurrected flesh, is the completion of a promise of salvation from long ago. Your promise is fulfilled, and we are nourished by your body until our time upon this earth has finished. Amen.

EASTER ACTION

Many churches have chapels containing the Blessed Sacrament for the sake of Eucharistic Adoration. Some of these are twenty-four-hour-a-day chapels to allow for around-the-clock adoration. Find a time to make a visit to the Blessed Sacrament sometime this week. If the experience is moving and deepens your spirituality, make time in your schedule for regular visits. Recognize the time you spend in the presence of Blessed Sacrament as sacred time, that is, God's time to work in you and through you.

*D*ay
51

Easter Thursday
Full Faith

irst, Sacred Scripture itself contains a path towards full faith in the resurrection of the dead. This is expressed as faith in God as creator of the whole man, soul and body, and as faith in God the Liberator, the God who is faithful to the covenant with his people. The Prophet Ezekiel, in a vision, contemplates the graves of the exiled which are reopened and whose dry bones come back to life thanks to the breath of a living spirit. This vision expresses hope in the future "resurrection of Israel," that is, the rebirth of a people defeated and humiliated (see Ezekiel 37:1–14).

Francis' General Audience, St. Peter's Square,
December 4, 2013

Scripture

The hand of the LORD came upon me, and he led me out in the spirit of the LORD and set me in the center of the broad valley. It was filled with bones. He made me walk among them in every direction. So many lay on the surface of the valley! How dry they were! He asked me: Son of man, can these bones come back to life? "Lord GOD," I answered, "you alone know that."

EZEKIEL 37:1–6

Prayer

Risen Christ, my bridge to eternal life, breathe your spirit into me now during my earthly life. When I am weary, when I am anxious, or when I am hardhearted, breathe your spirit into me; energize me and rejuvenate me, Lord, this I pray. I was born into new life with you through my baptism and I desire to share eternal life with you when I pass from this world—but sometimes I lose my way. Center me, O loving Jesus, on your Sacred Heart. May I be enlivened by your love, may it fill me to the point that there is no room for anxiety, apathy, or weariness. May I remain by your side until my dying day and beyond. Amen.

Easter Action

In what ways do you attempt to jump-start or rejuvenate your spiritual life when you feel it is waning? Does participating in the Mass renew your spirit? Do periods of quiet prayer (opening a silent space inside of you for God to speak) benefit you? Perhaps jumping into some kind of service to another helps. Write down what you do (or could do) to reenergize your faith life.

Day

52

Easter Friday
Resurrection and Life

*J*esus has come among us, he became man like us in all things, except sin; in this way he took us with him on his return journey to the Father. He, the Word Incarnate, who died for us and rose again, gives to his disciples the Holy Spirit as a pledge of full communion in his glorious Kingdom, which we vigilantly await. This waiting is the source and reason for our hope: a hope that, if cultivated and guarded—our hope, if we cultivate and guard it— becomes a light that illumines our common history.

FRANCIS' GENERAL AUDIENCE, ST. PETER'S SQUARE,
DECEMBER 4, 2013

SCRIPTURE

> *Jesus told her, "I am the resurrection and the life; whoever believes in me, even if he dies, will live, and everyone who lives and believes in me will never die. Do you believe this?" She said to him, "Yes, Lord. I have come to believe that you are the Messiah, the Son of God, the one who is coming into the world."*

JOHN 11:25–27

Prayer

Lord Jesus, risen Christ, even after her brother had died and Martha was dealing with that grief and her disappointment, she still remained strong in her faith. Martha knew that death was not the end. Martha knew that Jesus was Lord of all things and had control over every facet of the universe, including life and death. May we, Lord Jesus, share in Martha's faith and rest in the knowledge that you oversee every aspect of our lives with care and concern for every second of our earthly lives. Amen.

Easter Action

What relationships or people in your life test your faith? Write for ten to fifteen minutes about one or two relationships in your life that test your ability to follow God's will and display the love that Jesus modeled for those who believe in him. What qualities do the people you've selected possess that make it difficult for you to respond in a Christian manner? What are your "Christian coping strategies" for these people? Do you ignore them? Do you engage them in conversation? Do you pray for them? Do you pray for yourself? Review what you have written and pray on it.

Day

53

Easter Saturday
We Will Rise Again

The resurrection of us all will take place on the last day, at the end of the world, through the omnipotence of God, who will return life to our bodies by reuniting them to our souls, through the power of Jesus' resurrection. This is the fundamental explanation: because Jesus rose we will rise; we have the hope of resurrection because he has opened to us the door of resurrection. And this transformation, this transfiguration of our bodies is prepared for in this life by our relationship with Jesus, in the Sacraments, especially in the Eucharist. We, who are nourished in this life by his Body and by his Blood, shall rise again like him, with him, and through him.

FRANCIS' GENERAL AUDIENCE, ST. PETER'S SQUARE,
DECEMBER 4, 2013

But now Christ has been raised from the dead, the firstfruits of those who have fallen asleep. For since death came through a human being, the resurrection of the dead came also through a human being. For just as in Adam all die, so too in Christ shall all be brought to life, but each one in proper order: Christ the firstfruits; then, at his coming, those who belong to Christ.

1 CORINTHIANS 15:20–23

PRAYER

Lord Jesus, risen Christ, your resurrection makes my resurrection possible; you have conquered death on behalf of mankind. God has made himself incarnate, he has sanctified the flesh, he has suffered, died, and he has been resurrected—this is the story of salvation; all for the depth of love you have for your people (for me!). Lord Jesus, I know you are waiting for me and, until that day when I join you in paradise, I will endeavor only to do your will—and by your grace it will be done. Amen.

The Acts of the Apostles, which follows the four Gospels, chronicles how the apostles responded to the supreme sacrifice of the risen Christ. Explore how the apostles reacted to the wondrous news of the reestablishment of communion between God and man. What did they do with this newfound energy and excitement provided by their Lord and Savior? Take time today or tomorrow and begin to read this informative, moving, and invigorating book of the Bible. Become inspired by what the earliest Christians did in response to being saved by Jesus Christ.

$\mathcal{D}$ay
54

First Sunday After Easter
We Are Already Raised

I f it is true that Jesus will raise us at the end of time, it is also true that, in a certain way, with him we have already risen. Eternal life has already begun in this moment, it begins during our lifetime, which is oriented to that moment of final resurrection. And we are already raised, in fact, through Baptism; we are inserted in the death and resurrection of Christ and we participate in the new life, in his life. Therefore, as we await the last day, we have within us a seed of resurrection, as an anticipation of the full resurrection which we shall receive as an inheritance.

Francis' General Audience, St. Peter's Square,
December 4, 2013

Scripture

[Baptism] saves you now. It is not a removal of dirt from the body but an appeal to God for a clear conscience, through the resurrection of Jesus Christ, who has gone into heaven and is at the right hand of God, with angels, authorities, and powers subject to him.

1 Peter 3:21–22

Prayer

Jesus, Lord and Savior, I have already participated with you in your resurrection through my baptism. I am sharing in your glory right now, helping to build up the kingdom of God on earth. It is my earthly practice run, establishing good habits (virtues) and avoiding bad habits (vices). You are by my side every step of the way, gracing me with the power I need to choose wisely. When all is said and done, I am left with a rich and overwhelming sense of gratitude. This is not enough to suffice for all the love you have shown me, but all I have to express as a human being, along with my loving service to others in whom I see your loving face. Amen.

Easter Action

The days and weeks of Lent are an excellent period of time to get in shape, spiritually speaking. Just as athletes prepare their bodies in the weeks prior to their upcoming sports seasons, so we exercise with regular prayer, Mass attendance, the sacrament of reconciliation, increased self-denial, and consistent service to others. Write for five or ten minutes on how your relationship with your Lord and Savior, Jesus Christ, has been strengthened by your prayer and spiritual activity during this Lenten and Easter season.

CPSIA information can be obtained
at www.ICGtesting.com
Printed in the USA
LVOW01s2229200116
471622LV00019B/406/P